MARCO POLO
WESTERN CANADA
BRITISH COLUMBIA·ALBERTA

with Local Tips

*The author's special recommendations are
highlighted in yellow throughout this guide*

There are five symbols to help you find your way around this guide:

★

Marco Polo's top recommendations – the best in each category

☆

sites with a scenic view

◉

where the local people meet

👤

where young people get together

(100/A1)
pages and coordinates for the road atlas
(U/A1) *coordinates for the city map of Vancouver inside back flap*
(O) *outside area covered by the city map*

MARCO ⊕ POLO

Travel guides and language guides in this series:

Algarve • Amsterdam • Australia • Berlin • Brittany • California
Channel Islands • Costa Brava/Barcelona • Costa del Sol/Granada
Côte d'Azur • Crete • Cuba • Cyprus • Eastern USA • Florence • Florida
Gran Canaria • Greek Islands/Aegean • Ibiza • Ireland • Istanbul • Lanzarote
London • Mallorca • Malta • New York • New Zealand • Normandy • Paris
Prague • Rhodes • Rome • Scotland • South Africa • Southwestern USA
Tenerife • Turkish Coast • Tuscany • Venice • Western Canada

French • German • Italian • Spanish

*Marco Polo would be very interested to hear your
comments and suggestions. Please write to:*

North America:
Marco Polo North America
70 Bloor Street East
Oshawa, Ontario, Canada
(B) 905-436-2525

United Kingdom:
World Leisure Marketing Ltd
Marco Polo Guides
Newmarket Drive
Derby DE24 8NW

*Our authors have done their research very carefully, but should any errors or omissions
have occurred, the publisher cannot be held responsible for any injury, damage
or inconvenience suffered due to incorrect information in this guide*

Cover photograph: Rocky Mountains, Moraine Lake (Erich Bach Superbild/Ducke)
*Photos: Amberg (25, 58, 67); Author (10, 13, 15, 16, 18, 22, 35, 37, 38, 42, 46, 48, 55, 69, 70,
82, 84, 86); Jung (8, 29, 52, 80); Lade: Don (26), Lange (21, 72); Mauritius: Crader (60),
Hubatka (99); Schuster: Ikeda (45), Schmied (7), Tovy (4), Waldkirch (30); Timmermann (78)*

1st edition 1999
© Mairs Geographischer Verlag, Ostfildern, Germany
Author: Karl Teuschl
Translation: Jane Sutton
English edition 1999: Gaia Text
Editorial director: Ferdinand Ranft
Chief editor: Marion Zorn
Cartography Road Atlas: © SGA Ltd. (Map Art), Canada
Design and layout: Thienhaus/Wippermann
Printed in Germany

CONTENTS

Introduction: Discover Western Canada! 5
*The romance of the lumberjack, wild, wave-lashed beaches
and marvellous mountain panoramas – the new West is an
ideal holiday destination*

History at a glance 9

Canada in context: From bears to totem poles 11
*How lumber and oil brought wealth to Western Canada – some
interesting background details to help you understand the country*

Food & drink: Coffee shops and Western bars 19
*Canada's culinary charm lies in the diversity of regional
ingredients and the recipes brought to the country by immigrants*

Shopping & souvenirs: Native art 23
*Indian carvings and Inuit sculptures are popular and expensive,
but there are lots of other things ...*

Events: Rodeos and pioneer festivals 27
*Sporting events and humorous parades
are at the heart of most festivals*

Vancouver: The fairest in the land 31
*Sea and mountains set the scene for the metropolis
of Western Canada*

Victoria/Vancouver Island: Whales and rain forests 39
*Long beaches and deep green fjords give the West Coast
its own special charm*

British Columbia: Between the Rockies and the Pacific 49
*Magnificent mountains, beautiful lakes, colourful pioneer towns:
B.C. has got it all*

Rocky Mountains: On the dream highway of the world 61
*The Rocky Mountains are the home of the most –
and the most beautiful – National Parks in Canada*

Alberta: Country of wheat and forests 73
*The wide prairies of Alberta
oil reserves and dinosaurs*

The Northern Territories: On the trail of Jack London 83
The Arctic, one of the last wilderness regions on earth

Routes in Western Canada 89

Essentials: Practical information 93

Do's and don'ts 98
Some hints about possible dangers and things you should avoid

Road Atlas of Western Canada 99

Index 111

What do you get for your money? 112

Discover Western Canada!

The romance of the lumberjack, wild, wave-lashed beaches
and marvellous mountain panoramas —
the new West is an ideal holiday destination

Europeans may think they know Canada. It's on the same latitude as Central Europe, the climate is pretty similar, the mountains look like the Alps, the coastline looks like Norway's fjords. But Western Canada is different — more massive, more impressive, more isolated. What's missing are the people, the herdsmen's cabins on the mountains or the cable cars up to the mountain peaks.

There are no noisy motorways and the countryside is largely un-inhabited. Nor are there hedges and small fields. Instead, there is endless open space, and a hike up one of the mountain peaks — it doesn't matter where — offers a tremendous view over a landscape without streets or houses. Nature here has remained largely unchanged by man — it's

Icefields Parkway
in Banff National Park

the untouched world you dream about. Europe must have been like that once.

The first thing you have to get used to are the sheer dimensions of this country. A quick 50 km (30 mi) trip to the next shop or to a restaurant is quite normal and not even worth mentioning. Western Canada — the provinces of Alberta and British Columbia, the Yukon Territory and the western part of the Northwest Territories — covers a good three million sq km. The province of British Columbia alone, with an area of just 950,000 sq km or 336,800 sq mi, is about four times the size of Britain.

The West is ideal if you are travelling to Canada for the first time. It offers the most diverse scenery and beautiful contrasts. In the far west, the glacier-topped Coast Mountains, with their ancient and mysterious rain forests rise up from the dark wa-ters of the fjords of the Pacific coast, the habitat of whales and king salmon. Further inland, sheltered from the rain by the mountains, the high plateaus stretch away in the sun with their forests and lakes, frequently interrupted by a chain of mountain ranges, as far as the Rocky Mountains. These mountains contain the country's most beautiful national parks, Banff and Jasper, linked by Icefields Parkway, a spectacular panoramic road. Further to the east, on the other side of the Rockies, is Alberta's ranch country, where dinosaurs lived 60 million years ago, as proven by the many fossils found along Red Deer River. Today large herds of cattle graze here — in peaceful harmony with the oil pumps that carry Alberta's black gold. And finally, the mountain ranges and high valleys of the Yukon Territory and the Northwest Territories, covered with scant grass, stretch away to the far north. Only a hundred years ago this area was the scene of the biggest gold rush in history — today it is largely deserted again.

The climatic contrasts are just as diverse as the scenery. On the Pacific Coast there is a mild, damp maritime climate, while inland Canada has a continental climate, with hot summers and bitterly cold winters. High up in the Arctic North, summer lasts barely two months, while in the South, on the same latitude as Cornwall, in the Okanagan Valley in British Columbia, wine and peaches are grown. Yet even the extreme heat of the summer in the Alberta prairies and the polar cold in the wintery Arctic are tolerable because of the low humidity.

Just about 30 million people live in this huge country of Canada, and only six million of them in the Western priovinces. Statistically, this amounts to a population density of only 0.5 inhabitants per sq km (0.2 per sq mi) — in Central Europe, it is 400 times higher! That leaves a lot of space for camping, fishing, hiking, canoeing and riding. However, it isn't all wilderness. The metropolitan cities of the West, with their restaurants and their rich cultural life, are quite impressive. In fact, Vancouver, surrounded by water, is one of the most beautiful cities in North America and can easily compete with San Francisco. Prosperous, picturesque Victoria is more like a spa town than a provincial capital. On the sunny east side of the Rockies are the cities of Alberta, oil-rich Calgary, and Edmonton, the gateway to the North.

These cities are the only enclaves of modern civilisation in the far West, however. Only in the South, the region along the border with the USA, does one find development in the form of highways and settlements. Close to 80 percent of the population live in the fertile valley of the Fraser River, in the warm valleys around Kelowna and Kamloops and in the Alberta prairie. In contrast, the North of the provinces and the Arctic regions are almost empty of people. This helps explain the almost unbelievable friendliness and helpfulness of the people in western Canada — even in the very busy tourist centres in the Rockies. Western Canadians are always pleased to welcome visitors. After all, the days of the pioneers, when one was happy to see another human being, are not such a distant memory here.

The mountain scenery of Lake Louise in Banff National Park

Western Canada is the newest part of the country – historically as well as geographically. It was only 30 million years ago that the Rocky Mountains rose up out of the sedimentary strata of the primeval seas. The continental drift, during which the Pacific plate crashed against the North American mainland plate, formed the mountain ranges of the Cordilleras. Some 35,000 years ago, the ancestors of the Indians migrated across the Bering Straits and through western Canada, exploring and settling the continent from there. Their descendants are still the biggest ethnic group in the West. The Indians continue to live in their old tribal territories in small villages, asserting their rights with increasing political awareness. Their totem poles and magnificent longhouses can still be found and admired in many places, particularly along the West Coast.

It was not until much later, i.e. about 200 years ago, that the first white explorers, British sea captains James Cook and George Vancouver, sailed along the West Coast and started to trade in furs with the inhabitants. And it was only 100 years ago that the first cities were founded and the first railroad train steamed west from Montreal. Fur traders and gold diggers opened up the wilderness. Around the beginning of this century, the first true settlers started to arrive: farmers which came mostly from the Ukraine, England, Germany and Scandinavian countries.

Not much has changed since then. Mining, ranching and fishing, the cultivation of wheat, and more recently ginseng, are still the most important economic activities in the south of the provinces. The still largely undeveloped north is dominated by forestry – which has torn large holes in the landscape in some places. But there are still enormous stretches of completely untouched and uninhabited land, some of which is under permanent protection, as are the almost 10,000 sq km (3900 sq mi) of Tweedsmuir Provincial Park. Now as before, western Canada is a true paradise for those who love nature and the wilderness.

In terms of tourism, Western Canada offers the visitor a highly developed infrastructure, with a good network of roads, clean hotels and motels and extremely helpful tourist offices, which can provide many useful tips for festivals and things to do in their particular area. Fascinating museums and colourful markets, excellent restaurants, jazz clubs and Western saloons guarantee that you will never run out of things to do in the cities. The breathtaking countryside outside the cities is dotted with remote lodges, hospitable guest ranches and fishing camps to ease your passage into the wilderness. The national parks are a particular attraction. These parks enclose some of western Canada's most spectacular scenery and serve to protect its vital ecosystem. The most beautiful are without doubt the parks in the Rocky Mountains, but all of them are worth visiting.

There are many opportunities for adventure, whether it's a canoe trip in British Columbia, a horse ride in Alberta's ranch country, a photo safari to the polar bears in the Northwest Territories or a white-water rafting tour in the Yukon Territory. However, you don't have to push yourself to the limits. A pleasant tour in a mobile home can also give you a taste of freedom and space.

Former headquarters of the Hudson's Bay Company: Fort Edmonton

History at a glance

Around 35,000 B.C.
Paleoindian hunters reach North America across the Bering Straits

1497 A.D.
Commissioned by the British, John Cabot becomes the first European in modern times to sail to North America and to reach Newfoundland

1535/1536
French explorer Jacques Cartier discovers the St. Lawrence river and is the first to use the name Canada. In the 17th century the French start to colonise the St. Lawrence valley

1670
London merchants found the Hudson's Bay Company. This fur trading company is given all the land west of Hudson Bay by the King of England

1763
During the Seven Years' War France loses its lands in the New World. Quebec becomes a British Crown Colony. In the following decades, fur traders explore the West

1778
British explorer James Cook discovers the West Coast

1792/93
Alexander Mackenzie is the first to cross the continent and to reach the Pacific

1867
The birth of Canada: The British North America Act unites the colonies of Quebec, Nova Scotia and New Brunswick to form the Dominion of Canada

1871
British Columbia joins the Canadian Confederation

1885
The Trans-Canada Railway from Montreal to Vancouver is competed. First Canadian National Park founded in Banff

1898
Gold rush on the Klondike. First oil found in Alberta

1931
Canada becomes a Sovereign State in the British Commonwealth

1942
Construction of the Alaska Highway begins

1962
The Trans-Canada Highway is completed

1988
Winter Olympics in Calgary

1995
In a referendum the people of Quebec decide by a narrow majority that the province should remain in the Confederation – the unity of Canada is saved

1997
The handing over of Hong Kong to China terminates an immigration wave which brought some 70,000 Chinese to Vancouver

From bears to totem poles

*How lumber and oil brought
wealth to Western Canada — some interesting background
details to help you understand the country*

Bears

No trip to Canada would be complete without an exciting bear story to tell once you're safely back home. There's quite a good chance you'll have one. There are three species of bear that are native to Canada: polar bears, black bears and grizzlies. Polar bears, which can weigh up to 600 kg (1320 lbs), are only found in the icy arctic. The shy grizzlies (ursus arctos horribilis) inhabit the remote high valleys of the Rocky Mountains, along the West Coast and in the Arctic Tundra. You are very unlikely to see either of these species on your holiday.

Not so the third bear species, the black bear. Curious and always hungry, these bears snuffle round campsites in the evening, chase a surprised walker out of

*The Kwakiutl Indians of
Alert Bay carve particularly
expressive totem poles*

their blueberry patch or step out in front of cars on the Highway. The utmost care is recommended. You should only take that much-coveted bear photo from a safe distance, put all food away at night in your car or mobile home where it can't be smelled, and wash up your plates immediately after eating to remove all those delicious steak smells.

Bears have an excellent sense of smell and good hearing but their sight is very poor. When you're walking into the wind, it's a good idea to make a noise of some sort — surprised bears can be very unpleasant.

Flora and fauna

The greater part of western Canada is in the region of boreal forests which stretch across the continent in a wide green ribbon. White and black spruce, pine and fir trees grow here. Stretching over a breadth of 1,000 km (620 mi) in a north-south direction, these vast forests are the home of bears, moose, several species of deer, lynx, porcupines, beavers and small rodents. To the north, in the Yukon and Northwest Territories, the forests turn into taiga and, eventually, treeless tundra. Only caribou, mountain hare and musk-oxen can live on the sparse lichens and mosses of this region. However, the large areas of freshwater are the feeding grounds for countless water fowl in summer.

The south and east of Alberta are still part of the great North American prairie. This region was originally a grass savannah, but because of its fertile soil it is now extensively ploughed and covered with enormous grain fields. The former home of millions of bison has become the breadbasket of Canada. Bison can only be found in only a few protected areas today.

Alpine flora flourishes in the Rocky Mountains. There are lots of wild flowers for the mountain goats and mountain sheep to feed on. And finally, rain forests proliferate on the western slopes of the Coast Mountains and on Vancouver Island, with Douglas firs up to 80 m (300 ft) tall, Sitka spruce, gigantic cedars and lush green ferns.

French Canada

France lost its colonies in the New World during the Battle of Quebec in 1759. However, the French settlers remained, and their descendants now make up almost 30 percent of the entire population of Canada. As in the past, most French Canadians live in the province of Quebec. However, some young men and women in particular are now moving West because of the better economic conditions.

In recent decades, the linguistic and cultural partition of the country has repeatedly caused political crises in Canada. Since the 1960s, the nationalist *Parti québécois* has called for the independence of Quebec from Canada. There have even been terrorist attacks by separatists. Referenda have been held twice on the subject: in 1980 and 1995. On both occasions, the majority of the population of Quebec came out against separation — albeit by a very small margin. However, as long as the separatists dominate in Quebec, the subject of separation will not be completely off the agenda.

Gold

The novels of Jack London firmly planted the exciting story of the Klondike gold rush in the mind of every young reader.

In fact, the search for the yellow metal played a particularly important role in Canada. The discovery of gold caused vast regions in the West to be developed and settled.

Around 1860, the gold rush enticed thousands of desperados into the Caribou Mountains. Thirty years later it was 'Gold in the Yukon!', and around 100,000 hopeful gold diggers made the long, difficult journey across Chilkoot Pass. They endured bitter winters in the ice and snow of the Coast Mountains to get to their Promised Land by spring. Gold to the value of 100 million dollars was unearthed there in just three boom years. Dawson City (30,000 pop.), became the biggest city west of Winnipeg.

Gold can still be found today — on the Klondike and in Yellowknife. However, there is even more gold in the hard granite rock of the Canadian Shield in eastern Canada. A good five million ounces are mined per year. Much of this gold is used to make the Maple Leaf Dollar, which is one of the most widely sold gold coins in the world.

Hudson's Bay Company

The beaver and the hat fashion in Europe are to be thanked for the development of Canada. The rodent's woolly under-fur was used in the 17th and 18th centuries to produce felt for top-hats, three-cornered hats and other varieties of headware. On May 2, 1670 King Charles II of England gave his cousin, Prince Rupert, and 17 London investors the charter for what was to become one of the biggest commercial empires in history. Its territory, Rupert's Land, covered almost four million sq km, it's trading area eventually comprised one twelfth of the surface of the entire Earth.

As they searched for more and more new beaver areas, the fur traders gradually opened up the huge country. Their forts later became cities, their trade routes highways. In 1870 the Hudson's Bay Company handed over its land for 300,000 £ to newly founded Canada. But the company kept its trading posts, and now a department store chain with the distinctive name of The Bay can be found in many parts of western Canada.

A modern-day 'gold digger' at Bonanza Creek near Dawson City

Indians and Inuit

The predecessors of the Indians travelled across the Bering Straits to North America during the Ice Age at least 35,000 years ago. Over the centuries, they spread across the continent. Independent cultural groups developed: semi-nomadic hunting tribes lived in the North, while the Iroquois and Hurons of the woodland cultures in Eastern Canada became sedentary and cultivated maize, beans and tobacco. The tribes of the plains culture in the prairies of what is now Alberta followed the large buffalo herds, while the rich food supplies of the West Coast allowed the Kwakiutl and Haida sufficient leisure time to become skilled woodcarvers. The predecessors of the present-day Inuit colonised the Canadian Arctic from Alaska around 1,000 years ago.

The first decades of contact with white people was not as traumatic for the natives of Canada as it was for their fellow Indians in the United States. The fur traders of Canada were dependent on the help of the Indians and therefore interfered very little with their way of life. Nevertheless, diseases brought from Europe decimated the Indian tribes. It was only with the colonisation of the West in the 19th century that the Indians were forced onto reservations. Thanks to modern-day improvements in health care, a good 600,000 Indians and 50,000 Inuit live in Canada today.

Their rights as the original inhabitants of the continent were recognised in the constitution of 1982. In light of this development and the increasing self-awareness of Canada's native peoples, many tribes in the North and West are demanding self-government and the return of their land and. The Inuit (or Eskimos, as they were called by the Indians) have achieved the most spectacular success in this area. They will get their own territory in the far North of Canada in 1999. It is to be called 'Nunavut,' which means 'our country.'

Modern architecture

In the last 30 years, post-modernism has reached the metropolitan cities of western Canada, and Canada can also boast its own architects of world renown: Arthur Erickson, born in Vancouver, was responsible for the sensitive design of the Museum of Anthropology at the University of British Columbia, the solid concrete pillars of which recall Indian longhouses. German born Ed Zeidler designed the Canada Place Congress Centre in Vancouver to resemble sailing ships at anchor, and the prize-winning architect Moshe Safdie was responsible for the highly spectacular round structure of the Public Library in Vancouver built in 1995.

National Parks

The forerunner of what is now Banff National Park was founded in 1885 'for the health, benefit and pleasure of the population of Canada'. It was the first in a long series of parks erstablished to protect some of the most beautiful and unspoilt regions of this huge country. The Park system, run by the Canadian Ministry of the Environment, plays a pioneering role

Alert Bay is one of the main centres for salmon fishing

worldwide, particularly in view of today's ecological considerations. There are 38 national parks, with a total area of more than 200,000 sq km (77,000 sq mi). More parks are planned, and by the year 2000 every ecologically significant region of Canada is scheduled to be protected in a national park.

The national parks are among the most popular holiday destinations in the country. Almost 30 million visitors come every year to wonder at the magnificent mountain regions of Banff and Jasper, the isolated lakes of La Mauricie or the fjords of Gros Morne. However, you have to abide by the rules: Animals must not be fed; no branches may be broken off. Picking a bunch of wild flowers can prove expensive: there is a fine of up to $500. Hunting is strictly forbidden, but you may obtain a licence to fish in the streams and lakes.

Natural resources and industry

Western Canada is extremely rich in natural resources. Oil, natural gas and oil slate are found at the foot of the Rocky Mountains in Alberta province. The large rivers of British Columbia provide unlimited energy. The mountains have deposits of lead, zinc, silver and other metals, and even diamonds have been discovered recently in the Northwest Territories. Agriculture also plays a role. The fertile prairies in the South of Alberta provide wheat; peaches and other fruit flourish in the sunny Okanagan Valley. The best beef cattle in the country graze on the eastern slopes of the Rockies and on the enormous ranches around Williams Lake — this is Canada's cowboy country.

Now as before, the industrial production centres are in the East of Canada — even today the West is still restricted to its role of sup-

15

plier of natural resources for the world economy. Every tenth job in the country is dependent on the timber industry – in British Columbia every fourth. To be a lumberjack is to be in a very well thought of profession.

Every year, 150 million cubic metres (5,295 million cubic feet) of timber are cut throughout Canada. Most of it ends up as newspapers on breakfast tables all over the world. The fact that this highly destructive lumbering is tantamount to plundering the by no means inexhaustable forests is increasingly recognised by the government. It is using reforestation campaigns and taxes on the timber industry to save Canada's forests for future generations.

Political system

Canada is a federal-style parliamentary monarchy in the British Commonwealth. The official head of State is the Queen Elizabeth who is also Queen of Canada, although her duties are only ceremonial. The ten Canadian provinces have extensive powers of self-government, particularly in education, cultural policies, health care and the utilisation of mineral resources. However the two very thinly populated Northern Territories are still largely governed from the federal capital, Ottawa. Large areas of the North are to be returned to the Indians and Inuit people in the next few years, after which they will govern them themselves.

The history of the Mounted Police is acted out in the Fort Macleod Museum

Royal Canadian Mounted Police

The red-coated *Mounties* are the best known symbol of Canada. They often appear at official events in their parade uniforms and feature on many souvenir photos. The Mounties are more than a colourful ornament, however. They are a highly trained federal police force, responsible for all those rural regions and towns that cannot afford their own police force – and there are many of these in the West.

The RCMP, a force of some 15,000 men and women, were founded in 1873. For decades the forts of the Mounties were the only outposts of civilization in the West. The law enforcers patrolled the Arctic on dog sledges and penetrated to the most remote gold digger camps on horseback and by canoe. Today you can still see Mounties in the flesh – as radar patrols on the highways, lecturing and fining anyone caught speeding.

Salmon

Five different species of salmon are found on the Pacific Coast of Canada. The biggest and best-known is the king salmon, also known as *spring salmon* or *chinook salmon*. A *king salmon* can weigh up to 45 kg (99 lbs), while the smallest species, the Chum salmon, only reaches 2.5 to 5 kilos (5.5 to 11 lbs). In keeping with their primeval life cycle, all Pacific salmon return to the rivers after several years in the open seas. As if in response to a secret signal, they swim in thousands upriver to the streams in which they were born. There they spawn and die. The fish can tell by the taste of the water exactly which stream they must return to.

The great spectacle of the salmons' run can also be seen every summer on the Fraser River and on Vancouver Island. The most spectacular *salmon run* takes place at the beginning of October in the Adams River at Kamloops when hundreds of thousands of dark red sock-eye salmon jostle through the knee-deep water.

Totem poles

Indian carvings have become quite fashionable. Totem poles covered with hideous faces and mythical beasts, beautifully carved and often brightly painted, can be found outside many government buildings and museums in Canada. Gaudy plastic imitations fill the souvenir shops. The totem poles have become a symbol of Indian culture. Originally this highly complex carved art form existed only in the culture of the Northwest Coast Indians, in the region between Vancouver Island and Southeastern Alaska.

The *totem poles* were not religious icons but prestige objects, used by clans or chiefs to show their power and wealth. To dedicate a new pole, a big party was held which increased the standing of the host family even more.

For decades the 'heathen carvings' were banned by the government and by missionaries, but now the art is seeing a revival that started with the renaissance of Indian culture in the 1960s. The most beautiful poles are to be found in the museums in Vancouver and Victoria. Or you can visit the Indian villages on the West Coast, where there are still lots of original poles, for instance in Alert Bay, Quadra Island or Hazelton.

Coffee shops and Western bars

Canada's culinary charm lies in the diversity of regional ingredients and the recipes brought to the country by immigrants

National dishes

There is no such thing as a Canadian national dish. The immigrant groups arriving from all continents were too diverse, and the country was too big. Thus it is the great variety of specialities that provides a sort of 'multicultural' culinary pleasure in Western Canada. In the cities of Vancouver und Calgary, Chinese food is always a good choice. In the prairies around Edmonton you can find some excellent Ukrainian restaurants, thanks to the immigrants from South-Russia. And in all the big towns you will find Indian, Italian and often German restaurants. Wherever you go there is no shortage of the typical dishes for which Western Canada is well known: all imaginable variations of steak and fresh salmon.

Of course you will also find the usual fast food monotony of burgers and hot dogs in Canada. But if you resist the neon signs

If you like 'traditional' food …

on the thoroughfares of the cities and look for the smaller restaurants advertising *home cooking*, the small fish restaurants on Vancouver Island, the rustic lodges in the wilderness or the ethnic restaurants in the cities, you are bound to be pleasantly surprised.

Regional food

It is probably rather presumptuous to talk about independent regional cuisines in Canada, with the exception of the traditional French cuisine of Quebec in the east of the country, of course. Nonetheless there are some regional specialities and culinary trends in the western parts of the country as well.

In Alberta you should try a steak – either in a restaurant or self-cooked at the campsite. The meat of the cattle roaming freely on the huge ranches is superlative, and the portions are designed for hungry lumberjacks. West of the Rocky Mountains, in the Pacific province of British Columbia, you will be tempted

19

by fresh seafood, served fresh off the boat everywhere on Vancouver Island and along the Sunshine Coast north of Vancouver. A plateful of poached or grilled salmon (preferably silver salmon) with fresh vegetables from the Fraser Valley is among the greatest delicacies Canada has to offer.

Influenced by the trailblazing *California Cuisine,* which was invented in San Francisco and Los Angeles in the seventies, a new *Pacific Northwest Cuisine* has developed in Vancouver and Victoria in particular. It incorporates cooking styles and spices from all over the world – from France to the Far East. However, the raw ingredients are native to the area: salad from the Fraser Valley, sweet peaches, apples and grapes from the Okanagan Valley, crabs, halibut and salmon from the Pacific right at the doorstep.

In the better restaurants serving *Northwestern cuisine* the plates are often filled with unusual but very exciting combinations, such as pizza with smoked salmon or glazed crab with Thai curry dip. Rest assured that the talented young chefs know what they're doing. They have learned to harmonise the different tastes, and sometimes they still use very traditional methods: The salmon may be grilled, Indian-style, on wooden boards, and for dessert they may serve soapolallie ice-cream with wild berries from the local forest.

Restaurants

Breakfast is usually taken at the coffee shop which may be part of your hotel or located close to your motel. You can choose a between a *continental breakfast* (juice, coffee, toast and jam) and a more substantial *American breakfast,* which will often keep you going the whole day. The latter will include eggs – scrambled, boiled or fried (*sunny side up* or *over-easy*), bacon or ham and hash browns, with toast and jam on the side. You should also try *French toast* or an omelette. Coffee, which is usually weak (bet-

Do you fancy bear ham or moose steaks?

When you're in a wild country which is so close to nature as Canada is, you might expect to find tender wild duck or juicy moose steak on the menu quite often. But you would be wrong. Unlike in Europe, the sale of wild game is prohibited by law in both the United States and throughout Canada, and restaurant exemptions are rare. As a result, the Canadians hunt for their own consumption exclusively, and the only chance you may have to eat wild game is if you receive a private dinner invitation. The hunting season is in autumn, which means that by the time the next visitors arrive in spring, all the juicy bear steaks have already been cooked and eaten.

ter for your heart) is topped up free of charge for as long as you want. For lunch, served between noon and 2 pm, the Canadians often eat only small meals usually listed on a separate lunch menu: *Caesar's salad* or *soup and sandwich,* for example. You may also enjoy the large salad buffet or try a home-made hamburger which is often very good.

Dinner is usually served between 5.30 pm and 7 pm in rural areas and from 7 pm to 10 pm in the bigger cities. You are generally shown to your table. There is usually a sign at the entrance which reads: *Please wait to be seated.* Almost everywhere, smokers are put in a separate area, somewhere at the back of the restaurant.

The prices on the menu do not include a tip or the tax, which may vary from one province to the next. The tax, once added, will be shown on the bill. You are expected to leave the tip, normally 15 to 20 percent of the total bill, right on the table.

Drink

If Canada has a national drink, it must be beer — a very pleasant, fruity beer (compared with the watery US beer) that goes well with a hearty steak. Brands such as *Molson Canadian* or *Labatt's Blue* are available all over the country while some of the more special brews such as *Kocanee* are only found in a few regions and in the larger bars. Wine is often only available in the better restaurants, which usually offer good Californian wines. Native wines from the Okanagan Valley or the Niagara

An Indian woman baking bread in the traditional way

Peninsula are usually available everywhere too. If you want a stronger drink, try the excellent Canadian whisky, either with ice *(on the rocks)* or served with a mixer in the same way as rum or gin. A characteristic speciality of the North is Yukon Jack, a reelingly strong whisky liqueur for the long cold winter nights. In Western Canada, you will not only find the usual hotel bars, but also a great variety of country-style bars with pool tables and long counters. These are often the best places for meeting the *locals.* Something unique to Canada are the *cabarets:* they are not cabarets as such, but large bars with a stage where country bands appear most weekends.

Native art

Indian carvings
and Inuit sculptures are popular and expensive,
but there are lots of other things …

The West of Canada is not the obvious venue for a shopping trip but once you're there, there's something to tempt everyone to buy. First of all: leisure clothing, sports shoes and sports items in particular are much cheaper than in Europe, for example, and you can often get very good bargains at the frequent sales in the chain stores and shopping centres.

There are spacious and modern shopping centres, department stores and boutiques in all the big cities, like along Robson Street or in the Stephen Street Mall in Calgary. To avoid the bitterly cold winter weather, the Canadians have built entire shopping districts under cover, like for example the wonderful West Edmonton Mall. This is the biggest shopping mall in the world, with at least 800 shops, a mini-golf course, a large amusement park and an artifical lake complete with real submarines.

But this doesn't mean you have to stay inside in summer as

Enormous:
West Edmonton Mall

well. As part of the urban development programme, the old run-down port areas, which were becoming a bit of an eyesore, have been developed extensively over the recent decades. So developers have converted Granville Island in Vancouver and Victoria's old town into very popular and chic shopping and browsing areas, with art galleries and street cafes.

Pretty well only the nationwide chains are found in the big shopping malls. Department stores such as The Bay, along with a lot of smaller shops from the sportswear, shoe, book and toy chains. More individual shops, where you can buy novelty items and typical presents are more likely to be found in shopping streets in the cities or in the centres of the holiday resorts such as Jasper, Waterton, Chemainus or Tofino.

But one thing is true of all the shops: the customer is king. There is no shortage of sales staff who are generally unbelievably friendly. You only have to go into a shop and you will hear a friendly: *'Hi, can I help you?'*

Take them up on their offer – try the shoes in your size or the shirt in XL. Even if you end up not buying anything, the assistant won't be annoyed. The chat with an overseas visitor, no matter from which part of the world, will have been a pleasure.

Outside the cities the range of goods on sale generally decreases dramatically. A small general store which also sells shoes, power saws and spades has to cater for all your needs in many small places. So if you have decided to go on a long trip right across the country or up North, it is worth your while packing the camper full of all the necessary food and equipment. The further north you go, the more expensive it will become to purchase for all your daily needs. You also shouldn't forget to bring enough photographic equipment along from home!

Popular souvenirs

What are the best things to bring home? Not knick-knacks with 'Made in HongKong' stamped on underneath but typical Canadian products. Every supermarket sells the most widely known souvenir from Canada: *maple syrup.* The sweet, concentrated sap from the maple tree actually comes from the East of the country but it is part of every proper *pancake* breakfast in the West as well.

Some of the country's other typical products also make good souvenirs that are popular and tasty at the same time: jam from the Okanagan Valley for example or smoked salmon from the West Coast (you can also get this at Vancouver airport).

At the coastal resorts on Vancouver Island and in Vancouver itself you will find good-quality sailing equipment for yachting enthusiasts as well as beautiful, coarse knit Cowichan jumpers and all kinds of crafts made from wood, clay and ceramics. Many artists live on the Gulf Islands, particularly off Vancouver, and they generally exhibit their work in the galleries of Victoria. But beware. Many of the water colours and oilpaintings are nothing but mass-produced kitsch depicting rather cliché scenes with whales and coastal views.

Ideal souvenirs from Alberta are anything to do with cowboys: fine stetsons, silver belt buckles or hand-finished boots. Lots of Western shops offer a good selection, and you can even have your cowboy boots made to measure. You can find typical, large-checked lumberjack shirts everywhere in Alberta and British Columbia. They can be very useful on your travels round Canada as protection against the weather and the elements in general.

Some of the most beautiful, and unfortunately also the most expensive, souvenirs are the Indian and Inuit crafts. The tribes on the West Coast, once famous for their totem poles, now carve smaller items, such as bowls or masks, and transfer the expressive and stylised animal symbols of their traditional art to silver jewellery and drawings. Indians inland and in the North make traditional moccasins of moose leather, woven baskets decorated with porcupine quills and leather jackets embroidered with pearls.

Kitsch or art – the choice is huge

The Inuit in the Arctic are famous for their soapstone sculptures, which are also sold in the well-known galleries in Vancouver, Calgary and Whitehorse (prices from $300). Cheaper than the sculptures and just as popular as souvenirs are the colourful Inuit prints.

Another tip: it is best and safest to buy native arts and crafts direct from the Indians on the reservations rather than in the art galleries or in the museum shops in Vancouver, Victoria or Calgary.

Sizes and opening times

Canada converted to the metric system some years ago but you will still find American sizes widely used for clothing and shoes, because many of these products come from the USA. T-shirts and lumberjack shirts are usually only available in sizes *small, medium, large* and *X-large.* That's an easy choice. But you have to be more careful with off the peg dresses and trousers. For women US size 6 corresponds to 8 in British size. It's the same for men's shoes: US sizes are generally one size bigger than their British counterpart. If you're in any doubt, you can always ask any of the (generally very friendly) sales staff will and they will be glad to measure you.

Although most of the shops in the cities close around 6 pm, the supermarkets and the small shops at garages always stay open well into the night and in some cases even round the clock.

You can buy small items such as postcards, magazines, newspapers, etc in the *convenience stores* of the larger hotels between 7 am and 9 pm.

Rodeos and pioneer festivals

*Sporting events and humorous parades
are at the heart of most festivals*

Summer is the peak season for events in Western Canada. From May to September there are lots of smaller events as well as the big festivals in the cities. Every ethnic group and village celebrates for its own reasons: pioneer days, lumberjack competitions, rodeos and Indian powwows (dance festivals), as well as folklore and music festivals held by the various immigrant groups.

Find out from the local *Visitor Centre* where the next festivals are going to take place. The friendly atmosphere of the smaller rodeos in South Alberta or the small Indian festivals on Vancouver Island makes these events particularly charming. But watch out. Keep an eye on the dates of the bigger festivals, as hotels get very busy around the time of major events, such as the *Calgary Stampede.* You have to book a long time in advance.

Religious festivals make very little difference in Canada. In the cities many shops stay open with special sales. National holidays are traditionally on Mondays to give a long weekend – an opportunity for many Canadians to take a short holiday. Campsites and hotels in the popular holiday areas such as Okanagan Valley or Vancouver Island are often fully booked then. Two of these long weekends mark the beginning and end of the summer holiday season: *Victoria Day* at the end of May marks the start of the summer season with *Labour Day* weekend at the beginning of September marking the end.

OFFICIAL HOLIDAYS

Banks, schools, post offices and many museums are closed on the following days:

1 January *New Year's Day*
Easter *Good Friday* and *Easter Monday*
Monday before 25 May *Victoria Day*
1 July *Canada Day* (National holiday)
First Monday in August *Provincial holiday* in British Columbia and Alberta
First Monday in September *Labour Day*

Fantastic colours at a powwow, an Indian dance festival

MARCO POLO SELECTION: FESTIVALS

1 **Calgary Stampede**
Professional cowboys from all over the world come to Calgary for the biggest rodeo in the world (page 28)

2 **International Airshow**
A treat for all vintage aircraft fans at the town of Abbotsford (page 29)

3 **Klondike International Outhouse Race**
Nothing could be more crazy: a toilet race in Dawson City (page 29)

4 **Squamish Days**
Lots of outdoor types in sawing and wood chopping competitions. Just like the old days (page 29)

2nd Monday in October *Thanksgiving*
11 November *Remembrance Day*
25 and 26 December *Christmas*

FESTIVALS AND CELEBRATIONS

January
Vancouver: *Chinese New Year celebration with* Far Eastern masks and fireworks in Chinatown.

February
Whitehorse: *Sourdough Rendezvous* – a winter festival of the gold miners marking the start of the famous 1,500 km (940 mi) dog-sled race *Yukon Quest.*

Snow festivals and *carnivals* are held in many winter sports resorts (e.g. Banff, Kimberley and Nelson) in February and March, with ski races, costume parades and snow-shoe races and dog-sled competitions.

May
❖ Vancouver: *Children's Festival* with clowns und pantomimes.
Victoria: On *Victoria Day* colourful costume parades, concerts and vintage car races. The

following weekend sees the traditional *Swiftsure Race.*

June
Banff: Young artists get together from all over Canada from June until the end of August at the *Banff Festival of the Arts,* a series of concerts, plays and ballet performances.

Dawson City: On 21 June a big *Midsummer Night's* party on the Midnight Dome, the mountain above the city.

Vancouver: At the end of the month Chinese rowing teams enter in the *Dragon Boat Festival.*

July
❖ *Canada Day:* On 1 July picnics, parades and street parties are held almost everywhere in Canada. In the smaller towns and villages in particular the celebrations are often tremendous fun. Williams Lake celebrates the day with a *Rodeo,* Dawson City holds *gold panning competitions.*

Calgary: professional cowboys come here from as far away as Australia to take part in the ★ *Calgary Stampede,* which is the biggest rodeo in the world, held in the first two weeks of July.

Nanaimo: At the *International Bathtub Race* more than 100 fully equipped bath tubs race along the long and wet route to Vancouver.

Edmonton: *Klondike Days:* Pioneer festival with gold panning, boat races and Gold Rush style parades.

Edmonton: At the *Heritage Festival,* the biggest folk art festival in Canada, the many immigrants to Alberta demonstrate dances and crafts from their homelands. Last weekend.

Medicine Hat: Cowboys and farmers come from the distant prairies during the last weekend in July to the *Exhibition & Stampede,* where rodeos and chuckwagon races are held with lots of background country music.

August

Lethbridge: *Whoop-up Days.* The beginning of the month sees the famous rodeo with the obligatory Western music festival.

Squamish: ★ *Squamish Days Logger Sports.* Lumberjacks show their skills. First weekend.

Abbotsford: ★ *International Airshow:* old aeroplanes from all over North America.

Dawson City: *Discovery Days.* Around the 17th, celebrating the first gold found in the Yukon.

High River: *Chuckwagon Races* in the middle of the month.

Vancouver: *Pacific National Exhibition:* big annual fair.

September

Dawson City: On the first weekend the ★ *Klondike International Outhouse Race* sees all sorts of cleverly decorated toilets being pulled through the town by costumed gold diggers.

Prince George: *October festival:* The German immigrants celebrate their origins with lots of beer and brass bands during the last week in September.

Are sports really healthy? The Calgary Stampede

The fairest in the land

Sea and mountains set the scene for the metropolis of Western Canada

There could be no more beautiful introduction to a trip through the West than Vancouver (**100/C5**), 'Canada's Pacific pearl.' Vancouver is to the green West Coast of Canada what San Francisco is to the West Coast of the USA: a young and lively city with great charm, casual European flair and

A clock that hoots every quarter hour: the steam clock in the Gastown district of Vancouver

international spirit, a dynamic metropolis in a beautiful location with quaint Victorian rows of houses, all kinds of museums and attractions, spacious parks and lots of unspoiled nature all around. Vancouver is indisputably the most popular city in the entire region, a magnet for immigrants and visitors alike. The streets are filled with a colourful population from all nations – Asians in particular are well represented, as the Pacific trade

Hotel and Restaurant Prices

Hotels
Category 1: hotels and lodges over 150 Can$
Category 2: good hotels and motels under 150 Can$
Category 3: simple motels under 70 Can$

The rates are for two people sharing a double room.
As in the USA, single rooms in Canada are hardly any cheaper. Children usually share a room with their parents free of charge.

Restaurants
Category 1: over 40 Can$
Category 2: 25–40 Can$
Category 3: below 25 Can$
These prices are for an evening meal with soup or starter, main course and dessert.

Abbreviations
Av.	Avenue
Dr.	Drive
Hwy.	Highway
Mt.	Mount
Rd.	Road
St.	Street

MARCO POLO SELECTION: VANCOUVER

1 Bridges
Popular meeting places in the early evening – with fantastic views over the water and chic decor (page 35)

2 Canada Place
A relic of Expo '86: harbour promenade, cafes and lovely views (page 33)

3 Stanley Park
The most beautiful city park in Canada – ideal for a bicycle ride (page 34)

4 UBC Museum of Anthropology
Original totem poles and Indian masks by Northwest Coast Indians (page 34)

routes have resulted in a close relationship with the Far East for more than 100 years.

Vancouver's reputation as the most beautiful city in Canada is unchallenged. Surrounded by the sea, the urban scenery is offset by a dramatic backdrop of dark green mountains in the wide delta of the Fraser River. Several fjords reach deep inland, offering good anchorage for yachts and sea-going freighters. In addition, there are good beaches nearby. The reflections from glass towers mark the city centre, while carefully tended gardens dominate the suburbs.

The climate is uncharacteristically mild for Canada because of its proximity to the sea. But you can ski in the surrounding mountains in winter, while down in the city people are playing golf even in January. It is damp in Vancouver, however, and it rains a lot, especially in autumn and spring, while from July to September it is often sunny for weeks on end. There are very few visitors who won't say to themselves: I could spend a lot more time here. Accordingly, the rise in real estate prices has been steep – particularly since many wealthy Hong Kong Chinese crossed the Pacific to settle here before the Crown Colony was handed over to China.

With around 1.8 million inhabitants in the conurbation on the Fraser Delta, Vancouver is now the biggest city in Western Canada, and with more than 150 km (93 mi) of docklands it is Canada's most important economic and trading centre on the Pacific. Two famous universities, numerous museums, theatres and galleries make it the cultural centre of Western Canada. And in recent years so many films and television series have been filmed here that the city has become known as 'Hollywood North'.

Yet this dynamic metropolis – the third largest city in the whole of Canada – is still surprisingly young. There were only huge Douglas fir forests here when Captain George Vancouver discovered the mouth of the Fraser

River in the Pacific in 1792 — and sailed past. It was not until the year 1860 that a small lumberjack camp was set up on the shore of Burrard Inlet. John 'Gassy Jack' Deighton, who opened the first saloon back then, has since been considered the founder of the city. When in 1886 the terminus of the transcontinental railway was built here, the growth of Vancouver became unstoppable.

Trade with Eastern Asia flourished; the fishing and timber industries brought new jobs. A century later, at the World Exhibition in 1986, the city showed that it had become a metropolis which is pleasant to live in and close to nature, an oasis of urban culture in the middle of the remote wilderness of Western Canada.

SIGHTSEEING

You should put aside at least two days for Vancouver: one day for an extended stroll through the city centre, and another for a visit to the museums and attractions in the suburbs. A car is unnecessary for the city itself — the downtown area is very compact and the streets are often clogged with traffic anyway. The city centre, where most of the sights are to be found, is on a peninsula between Burrard Inlet and False Creek. You can take your first look from *The Lookout* at the ◢◣ *Harbour Centre* (**U/E4**) on Hastings Street or — for a better view — take a cablecar ride up to ◢◣ *Grouse Mountain* in North Vancouver (**O**).

The lively city centre is most uncharacteristic of North America: People crowd into the street cafes along busy *Robson Street* (**U/C3–D4**) to drink cappuccino, read and chat. Nearby on Robson Square the skateboarders try to leap up the steps, while below,m by the docks in the attractive old *Gastown* area (**U/E4**), visitors stroll past the galleries and souvenir shops. Directly to the east you'll find the smells and colours of the Far East in the constantly crowded streets of *Chinatown* (**U/F4**). You should also include half a day for *Stanley Park* (**U/A–D1**) with its wonderful ◢◣ views of the city skyline. And on a sunny day it's worth visiting the West End for the beaches on *English Bay* (**U/A3–4**).

Canada Place   (U/E3)

★ During Expo '86, the brilliant architect Ed Zeidler constructed a snowy white canvas roof over the pier of the Canada Pavilion. It's lovely strolling here today, watching the cruise ships and taking in the ◢◣ view of the port and the mountains from the cafe at the end of the pier. The IMAX cinema inside the building shows films about Canada.
Cordova St./Howe St.; cinema admission: $8–11.50

Capilano Suspension Bridge   (O)

A swaying, almost 140 m (460 ft) long ◢◣ suspension bridge over a 70 m (230 ft) deep canyon. Unfortunately it is also a tourist trap with a huge souvenir shop — but still exciting.
North Vancouver, Capilano Rd.; in summer daily 8 am–9 pm, otherwise 9 am–5 pm; admission: $8.95

Chinatown   (U/F4)

The area around Pender, Hastings and Main Streets is the biggest

Chinese community in North America after San Francisco. Good restaurants. The *Dr. Sun Yat-Sen Classical Chinese Garden* on Carrall Street, the only traditional Chinese garden in North America, is worth a visit.

Gastown (U/E4)

The old city of Vancouver has been restored along Water Street. The old brick buildings house shops, restaurants and art galleries. An interesting attraction is the *Steam Clock* on the corner of Cambie Street, which hoots every quarter and is operated by the city heating system.

Queen Elizabeth Park (O)

Beautiful park in an old quarry. Excellent ◁◁ panoramic view of Vancouver. A glass domed building at the top of the hill houses a small botanical garden.
Bloedel Conservatory. Cambie St./ 33rd Av.

Stanley Park (U/A–D1)

★ ◁◁ Magnificent city park surrounded by water, with trails and picnic sites. Aside from original *totem poles* you can also see the last *ancient Douglas firs* in the city centre. *Lions Gate Bridge,* built in 1938 at the north end of the park, formerly the biggest suspension bridge in the British Empire, links the city to North Vancouver. The small *zoo* in the middle of the 400 ha (1,000 acre) park is great for children in particular, the excellent *aquarium* nextdoor features beluga white whales, playful sea otters and an exhibition on the journey of the salmon. You can take the 10 km (6 mile) long *Stanley Park Drive* (one way) to go round the penin-

sula on which the park lies – best by *bicycle (on hire near to the park entrance on Denman St.).*

Vancouver Trolley

Perfect for sightseeing: The trolley buses drive along a fixed route past all the downtown attractions. You can get on and off where you want – there's a bus every 30 minutes. *Daily 9 am–6 pm; tickets $20*

MUSEUMS

Maritime Museum (U/A5)

The main attraction of this museum is the 'St. Roch', a Royal Canadian Mounted Police Arctic patrol ship. The old schooner is also interesting because it has travelled the Northwest passage through the Polar Sea several times.
1100 Chestnut St.; daily 10 am– 5 pm; admission: $6

Science World (U/F5)

The 'glass ball' at the East end of False Creek is one of the last relics of Expo '86. Today it houses a large technical museum, which also has a children's department and shows impressive films on a huge wrap-around screen.
1455 Quebec St.; daily 10 am–5 pm, Sat until 6 pm; admission: $13.50

UBC Museum of Anthropology (O)

★ The original museum building by Arthur Erickson on the site of the University of British Columbia houses an important collection of totem poles and masks by Northwest Coast Indians. Very beautiful historical carvings from argillite as well as modern works by Bill Reid. In summer occasional displays of Indian dancing. Very good museum shop.

Unusual architecture to arouse the curiosity: Canada Place

6393 NW Marine Dr.; daily 10 am–5 pm in summer; Tue– Sun 11 am–5 pm in winter; admission: $6

Vancouver Museum   (U/A5)

The large circular building on the shore of English Bay presents the history of the city of Vancouver, natural history and Indian crafts in a stimulating way. Attached is a Planetarium, which shows Lasershows in the evenings.

1100 Chestnut St.; daily 10 am–6 pm in summer, otherwise 10 am–5 pm; closed Mondays; admission: $5

Van Dusen Botanical Garden   (O)

22 hectares (55 acres) of flowers and woods, idyllic walks and small lakes. The garden is particularly colourful from May to July.

5251 Oak St.; daily 10 am to dusk; admission: $5.50

RESTAURANTS

A Kettle of Fish   (U/B5)

As the name suggests: fish in all variations. Popular and good.

900 Pacific St., Tel: (604) 682-6661; Category 2

Bridges   (U/B6)

★ ❖ Popular bistro. Bar and restaurant at the water's edge with views of city.

Granville Island, 1696 Duranleau St.; Tel: (604) 687-4400; Category 2

Doll and Penny's   (U/B4)

❖ ⚡ Trendy cafe in the West End, open until 2 am. Good place for breakfast, too.

1167 Davie St.; Tel: (604) 685-3417; Category 3

Floata   (U/E4)

An authentic Chinese restaurant in the bustle of the Chinese quarter. Tasty Dim Sum at lunchtime. It's a must.

180 Keefer St.; Tel: (604) 602-0368; Category 2

The Cannery   (O)

Excellent cooking (fish specially recommended here!) and lovely ❤️ panoramic view over the mountains and Lions Gate Bridge.

A bit further away in the port area, best reached by taxi.
2205 Commissioner St.; Tel: (604) 254-9606; Category 1

Water Street Cafe (U/E4)
Nice Italian bistro in the heart of Gastown.
300 Water St.; Tel: (604) 689-2832; Category 2–3

SHOPPING

The main shopping street is the lively *Robson Street* with its many street cafes and boutiques (**U/C–D 3–4**). To the North of Robson Square are the big department stores such as Eatons or The Bay. *Granville Island* and *Lonsdale Quay Market* (**O**) with their markets, cafes and small, original shops tempt the visitor to buy (smoked salmon!) or browse.

HOTELS

Blue Horizon (U/C3)
Tall hotel in the heart of the city centre. Very big rooms and ☆ good views from the upper floors.
214 rooms; 1225 Robson St.; Tel: (604) 688-1411; Fax: 688-4461; Category 2

Buchan (U/B2)
☆ Simple and cheap but clean hotel at the edge of Stanley Park.
61 rooms; 1906 Haro St.; Tel: (604) 685-5354; Fax: 685-5367; Category 3

Metropolitan (U/D3–4)
Elegant, somewhat older hotel in the centre, with perfect service and an excellent restaurant.
197 rooms; 645 Howe St.; Tel: (604) 687-1122; Fax: 643-726; Category 1

Pan Pacific Vancouver (U/E3)
Luxury hotel in ideal location on the edge of Gastown with fabulous ☆ view over the city and Burrard Inlet.
506 rooms; 999 Canada Place, Tel: (604) 662-8111; Fax: 685-8690; Category 1

Sylvia (U/A3)
Older, very charming middle category hotel in the West End, right on the beach in English Bay.
115 rooms; 1154 Gilford St; Tel: (604) 681-9321; no Fax; Category 2

SPORTS & LEISURE

Beaches
The water of the Pacific is relatively cool even in summer but the beaches on *English Bay* (**U/A3–4**) are good for paddling and sunbathing. The best beaches are west of the city centre on *Kitsilano Beach* and *Jericho Beach* (**O**).

ENTERTAINMENT

You will find up to date details of clubs and concerts in the weekly 'Georgia Straight', the monthly magazine 'Vancouver Guideline' and in the weekend edition of the 'Vancouver Sun'. Tickets for concerts, sports events and theatre productions are available from *Eaton Ticket Center* on Robson Square (**U/D4**) and at *Ticket-Master, 1304 Hornby Street* (**U/D4**), Tel: (604) 280-44 44. Downtown nightlife is concentrated in the West End around *Denman Street* and in the new trendy quarter of *Yaletown*.

Alma Street Cafe (O)
Popular jazz club in the bustling student quarter around 10th

Avenue west of the city centre.
2505 Alma St.

Bar None   (U/D5)
♣ Trendy bar in the old ware-
house district of Yaletown with
pool tables and a large selection
of beers.
1222 Hamilton St.

Chameleon   (U/D4)
❖ The big bar in the cellar of the
Georgia Hotel is particularly
popular with office workers on
their way home. Good beer and
atmosphere.
801 W Georgia St.

Joe Fortes   (U/C3–4)
Chic bar and restaurant – the
place to be seen.
777 Thurlow St.

The Shark Club   (U/D4)
❖ Typical Canadian sports bar
with large TV screens and lots
of atmosphere during football
matches. Mixed clientele.
*In the Sandman Hotel, 180 W
Georgia St.*

INFORMATION

Vancouver
Tourist Info Centre   (U/D3)
Multilingual staff. Bookings for
accommodations and sightseeing
tours.
*Waterfront Centre; 200 Burrard St;
Tel: (604) 683-2000; Fax: 682-6839*

SURROUNDING AREA

Fort Langley   (100/C5)
The old fur trading fort on the
Fraser River is approximately
50 km (30 miles) south east of
Vancouver on Highway 1 and
the historic site is worth a visit.

*Indian art without cliches in the
UBC Museum of Anthropology*

The 'inhabitants' of the post
wear the costumes of the era
and re-enact the harsh lives of
the trappers in the 19th century
for visitors.
*Langley; daily 10 am–5 pm; admis-
sion: $4*

Sunshine Coast   (100/C4)
Protected by the offshore islands
and in actual fact very sunny –
the coast north of Vancouver is
particularly suitable for a one or
two day visit to the deep green
fjords on the Pacific. From the
city, Highways 99 and 101 head
north to *Powell River,* car ferries
cross the fjords. Small yacht
ports, fishing villages and beach
parks like *Saltery Bay Provincial
Park* line the route. The large
B.C. Mining Museum in Britannia
Beach is a must.
*About 50 km (30 mi) from Vancou-
ver on Highway 99; July/Aug 10
am–4.30 pm daily, May/June and
Sept/Oct Tue–Sun 10 am–4.30
pm; Tel: (604) 688-8735; admission: $10*

Whales and rain forests

Long beaches and deep green fjords give the West Coast its own special charm

Relentlessly the rough Pacific beats against the tattered coast, the west winds bring rain-filled clouds across the sea. Whales and sea lions frolic in the dark waters of the bays; on land, Douglas firs and ancient Sitka spruces tower up in mysterious, dark forests. Vancouver Island — the biggest island on the West Coast of North America with a length of 450 km (280 mi) — is a world apart: a fascinating primeval world of deep fjords and mountains over 2000 m (7000 ft) high, with quiet bays and wildly romantic beaches.

The contrasts of the island are particularly enchanting: sleepy fishing villages, Indian reservations and lumber camps in the barely accessible North, busy holiday resorts and the elegant provincial capital, Victoria, in the South. Above all, the island is ideal for a holiday in and around nature. And not just for dedicated fans of the wild, either. The excel-

Nothing can be changed here:
Long Beach in
Pacific Rim National Park

lent infrastructure of remote campsites and lodges also make it suitable for mobile home holiday makers and families.

As yet only one road, Island Highway 19, runs along the entire island from south to north. For the most part it follows the east coast which is protected by a long mountain mass. The wild, rainy west coast, the site of Pacific Rim National Park with its unique rain forests, is still virtually inaccessible — a dream for those who love hiking and kayaking in the wild.

The mild East Coast on the other hand has been well developed and is known for its bathing beaches, as the calm water of the Strait of Georgia, which separates the island from the mainland, warms up to pleasant temperatures in summer. The southern end of the island has an almost frost-free climate almost all year round — as you can see from the beautiful gardens in Victoria's residential suburbs.

The huge wooded areas make Vancouver Island one of the most important forest regions in Canada — and the timber industry has frequently caused destruction and chaos in the ancient forests over the last 100 years. In the North in particular you frequently come across areas of complete deforestation. Yet for many in the region, felling is still the only possible source of income. It has only been in recent years, ever since the protests of the environmentalists have become louder, that the industry has started to consider more thoughtful felling methods. And most recently the provincial government has increased the level of protection for the ancient forests.

Travel details for a tour of Vancouver Island are quite simple: hourly connections with big car ferries from Tsawwassen and Horseshoe Bay travel between the mainland and the island. It is worth staying one or two days in Victoria. You need another two days to get to know the Pacific Rim National Park, and you should allow about a week for a trip to see the killer whales and Indian villages in the North. From Port Hardy you can press further north by ferry through the maze of islands which form the Inside Passage (advance booking is essential).

ALERT BAY

(100/B4) This little fishing village on a small offshore island (ferry service from Port McNeill) is the home of the Kwakiutl Indians, long known for their particularly expressive wood carvings. You can admire the brightly painted old totem poles all round the village square. The tribe's greatest legacy – old masks and decorated chests and poles, are shown in the U' Mista Cultural Centre.
Mon–Fri 9 am-5 pm; from May–Sept also on Sat and Sun 12 noon–5 pm; admission: $5

CAMPBELL RIVER

(100/B4) Keen anglers get excited when they hear the name of this small port. It is here, in the middle of Vancouver Island, that the biggest salmon in Canada are caught every summer. 30 kilo (65 lb) king salmon are by no means unusual. On the pier here you can admire the aficionados and their trophies. The water all round is dotted with numerous boats in high season. Quadra Island, which lies offshore, is a Kwakiutl Indian reservation.

MUSEUM

Kwagiulth Museum
★ This pleasantly laid out, modern museum is a real treasure trove of Kwakiutl Indian masks.
Cape Mudge, Quadra Island; in summer Mon–Sat 10 am–4.30 pm; admission: $3

HOTELS

Strathcona Park Lodge
Large, comfortable lodge on the shore of Upper Campbell Lake in the middle of Strathcona Park. Many sports available and good rates for hikers, canoeists and climbers.
46 rooms, P.O. Box 2160, Campbell River; Tel: (250) 286-3122; Fax: 286-6010; Category 2

Super 8 Motel
Simple motel at the southern end of the resort — but with a pool.

*39 rooms; 340 South Island High-
way.; Tel/Fax: (250) 286-6622,
Category 2–3*

Tsa-Kwa-Luten Lodge

Lodge run by Indians on Quadra
Island. You can stay in the large
rooms in the main building
which is decorated with carvings
or in log cabins on the sea shore.
*34 rooms; P. O. Box 460, Quathia-
ski Cove; Tel: (250) 285-2042,
Fax: 285-2532, Category 1–2*

SURROUNDING AREA

Strathcona Provincial Park (100/B4)

This extensive park high in the
mountains west of the Campbell River is of particular interest to hikers: a well developed
network of trails runs from the
two roads in the Park up into the
mountains. The trip to *Flower
Ridge* at the southern end of
Buttle Lake, to name only one
of these trails, is particularly
beautiful.

DUNCAN

(100/C5) This small town (5000
pop.) in the fertile Cowichan
Valley would not really have anything special to offer if the Cowichan Indians on the adjacent
reservation had not returned to
their traditions ten years ago,
founding a cultural centre and
starting to carve totem poles. All
along the streets in the town you
can now see brightly coloured
poles – highly thought of by the
white inhabitants as a money-
spinning tourist attraction.

MUSEUMS

B.C. Forest Museum

Everything about felling. From old
chain saws to a saw mill and a complete lumber camp – this open air
museum brings together everything to do with *lumberjacks*.
*At the Northern end of the town,
Hwy. 1; May–Sept daily 9.30 am–6
pm; admission: $7*

MARCO POLO SELECTION:
VANCOUVER ISLAND

1 Butchart Gardens
The most beautiful flowers
in the West — spread over
20 ha (50 acres) (page 47)

2 Kwagiulth Museum
Fantastic masks and totem
poles by Kwakiutl Indians
(page 40)

3 Pacific Rim National Park
Gigantic trees in the
Canadian rain forest and
wildly romantic beaches

along the West Coast
(page 43)

**4 Royal British Columbia
Museum**
Reproductions of rain
forests, Indian art
and pioneer history
(page 46)

5 Stubbs Island Charter
Visit to the Johnstone
Strait, habitat of the killer
whale (page 44)

In Chemainus, history speaks through 30 murals

Native Heritage Center

In their large cultural centre, the Cowichan Indians show visitors how they carve totem poles and weave baskets. Frequent dancing displays.

200 Cowichan Way; 9.30 am– 5.30 pm daily; admission: $7.25

SURROUNDING AREA

Chemainus (100/C5)

The former saw mill has become a holiday resort over the last ten years. More than 30 large murals by international artists illustrate the history of Vancouver Island and its people. During the summer there are craft exhibitions, street festivals and parades attracting visitors nearly every weekend. Slightly stereotyped perhaps but still worth the visit.

GULF ISLANDS

(100/C5) An archipelago of small islands lies between Vancouver Island and the mainland. *Saltspring, Galiano* and *Gabriola* are the biggest and can be reached by ferry from Swartz Bay or Nanaimo.

The climate here is particularly mild and sunny — palmtrees even grow in some parts! Artists, writers and craftsmen have decided to settle here — not least because of the contemplative lifestyle. It is best to do the islands by bicycle. You can hop quickly from island to island on the ferry and a bicycle is the best means of transport on the largely car-free islands.

NANAIMO

(100/C5) Nanaimo is the northern ferry port for ships to the mainland and a good starting point for trips to the middle section of the island. This city, the second biggest on Vancouver Island, awaits you with well-kept yacht harbours, a pretty harbour promenade and parks along the coast.

HOTEL

Tigh-Na-Mara Resort
A beautifully green space with log cabins and holiday apartments on the beach, slightly to the north of Nanaimo.
142 rooms; Parksville, 1095 E Island Hwy.; Tel: (250) 248-2072; Fax: 248-4140; Category 1–2

INFORMATION

Nanaimo Travel Infocentre
2290 Bowen Rd.; Tel: (250) 756-0106; Fax: 756-0075

SURROUNDING AREA

Parksville (100/B–C5)
The real charm of Nanaimo is found in the area around it: the most beautiful, and warmest, *beaches* on Vancouver Island stretch north around Parksville and Qualicum Beach. About a 20-minute drive inland on Highway 4 and you can admire the over 800-year-old Douglas firs and cedars in *MacMillan Provincial Park (*laid out trails).

PACIFIC RIM NATIONAL PARK

(100/B5) ★ One of the most beautiful and wildest sections of the West Coast has been protected in this just 400 sq km (155 sq mi) park: ancient rain forests, fissured rocks and beaches strewn with driftwood, like the 11 km (7 mi) long, in some places several hundred metres wide Long Beach.

In the *Museum and Visitor Center* on ⤳ Wickaninnish Beach you can hear the natural history of this region explained in great detail and with great competence. The friendly rangers are happy to give hiking advice to anyone who asks. Particularly impressive are the educational trails like the *Rain Forest Trail.* And don't forget this is rain forest — a waterproof cape is a must in this region.

For *kayak enthusiasts* the small archipelago of the Broken Islands Group is highly recommended. *Wilderness hikers* can spend an entire week on the 72 km (45 mile) West Coast Trail (advance booking is essential) from Port Renfrew to Bamfield — provided they are fit enough, of course. From Tofino, the small port at the northern end of the Park, you can take *boat trips* to remote bays and to watch the whales.

TOURS

Barkley Sound Service
The former freighter "M.V. Lady Rose" is now used as a ferry in Barkley Sound. Full day trips from Port Alberni to Ucluelet and Bamfield. Also takes hikers to the West Coast Trail and kayakers to the Broken Islands Group.
Book in advance if it's possible: P. O. Box 188, Port Alberni, B.C. V9Y 7M7; Tel: (604) 723-8313

Chinook Charters
Motor boat and dinghy trips to watch the whales off the West Coast and to the hot springs on a remote island. The best time to watch the grey whale is in the spring.
450 Campbell St., Tofino; Tel: (604) 725-3431

HOTELS

Pacific Sands Beach Resort
Quiet, well-kept hotel, right on the shore. 10 log cabins with open fires.
54 rooms; P.O. Box 237, Tofino; Tel: (250) 725-3322; Fax: 725-3155; Category 1–2

Wickaninnish Inn
Holiday hotel with a wonderful location on the cliffs, with beach and nice restaurant.
46 rooms; Tofino, Chesterman Beach; Tel: (250) 725-3100; Fax: 725-3110; Category 1

INFORMATION

Pacific Rim National Park
P.O. Box 280, Ucluelet, B.C. V0R 3A0; Tel: (250) 726-7721

PORT HARDY/ INSIDE PASSAGE

(100/A4) Port Hardy, a port (5300 pop.) at the northern end of Vancouver Island, is the starting point for the legendary Inside Passage, the watery route through the fjords of the West Coast, which the Gold Diggers sailed to the Yukon Territory and through to Alaska 100 years ago. Not much has changed since then: green bays and mountains dominate the scenery, and there is the occasional lighthouse. The scenery is wild and magnificent and surely one of the highlights of any visit to Canada. The 15 hour trip by *car ferry from Port Hardy to Prince Rupert or Bella Coola* should be booked well in advance through a travel agent at home. *Info: Tel: 1-(888) 223-3779.*

HOTEL

North Shore Inn
Good for one night in transit: a big, reliable motel, with beautiful ❀ views of the bay from all rooms. Steak restaurant and ✪ Bar, where there are often country bands playing.
Port Hardy, 7370 Market St., Tel: (250) 949-8500, Fax: 949-8516, Category 2

TELEGRAPH COVE

(100/B4) The tiny fishing village south of Port McNeill with just 12 inhabitants has become a mecca for whale watchers and whale researchers in recent years. Several groups of killer whales live here in the protected salmon filled waters just off the the coast.

TOURS

North Island Forestry Centre
The Canadian timber industry is to improve its image: very informative (if slightly partial) tours through the sawmills, lumber camps and felling areas. You should book the free tours a few days beforehand.
Port McNeill; Tel: (250) 956-3844

Stubbs Island Charter
★ From June to October half-day boat trips into the Johnstone Strait, a reserve for orcas (killer whales).
Telegraph Cove; Tel: (250) 928-3185; tickets: $60

VICTORIA

(100/C5) The capital of the province of British Columbia

(310,000 pop.) basks in the colonial legacy of the British Empire — with neat gardens, Victorian architecture and horse-cabs for sightseeing. English afternoon tea in the ivy clad Empress Hotel, one of the landmarks of the city, is a popular attraction. The mild climate (ideal for golf) and its water-locked location on the Juan de Fuca Strait make Victoria one of the most popular holiday resorts in the West.

Victoria has been the capital of British Columbia since 1871, only 30 years after it was founded as a trading post of the Hudson's Bay Company. But the small city has never really become a metropolis. The former pioneer settlement has turned into a peaceful city of civil servants. In recent decades very wealthy senior citizens

have settled here to spend their retirement years playing golf in the fine weather. More recently they have been joined by young sailing enthusiasts, who appreciate the many leisure possibilities offered by the city.

SIGHTSEEING

A must for tourists is a walk in the *Inner Harbour,* full of sailing boats and yachts, around which the main attractions of the city are grouped. On the east side of the harbour is the traditional *Empress Hotel,* on the northern side is the *old town* with its shopping streets and small passages. The south side is dominated by the splendid *Parliament building* dating back to the year 1898. In front of this — as in many other places — is a statue

The majestic Empress Hotel on the Inner Harbour in Victoria

of Queen Victoria. At night the building is illuminated by lots of small lamps – a bit over the top maybe, but very impressive.

You should also visit *Beacon Hill Park* to the south of Inner Harbour. Here, at the foot of Douglas Street, is the end of the famous Trans-Canada Highway, which starts 7,821 km (4,890 mi) to the east in Newfoundland. From the park you can drive along ◁◁ *Scenic Marine Drive,* which follows the coastline northeast through residential suburbs like Oak Bay.

MUSEUMS

Craigdarroch Castle
The most beautiful Victorian building in the city. Scottish coal magnate Robert Dunsmuir had this country house built in 1890. *1050 Joan Crescent; in summer daily 9 am–7 pm; otherwise 10 am–4 pm; admission: $ 7.50*

Miniature World
Your children will be enchanted: a museum full of dolls houses and miniature scenes from fairy tales and children's stories.
In the Empress Hotel, Humboldt St.; in summer daily 8.30 am–9 pm; otherwise 9 am–5 pm; admission: $7

Royal British Columbia Museum
★ You should set aside at least half a day for the biggest museum in the province. Realistic reproductions of rain forests and fjord coastlines are on display, as are wonderful totem

Colourful flowers almost the year round: Butchart Gardens

poles and exhibitions on pioneer history. It is highly recommended. There is an excellent shop right in the museum.
675 Belleville St.; in summer daily 9 am–5 pm; admission: $6.50

RESTAURANTS

Don Mee
Cantonese food in the heart of Chinatown.
538 Fisgard St., Tel: (250) 383-1032; Category 2

Swan's Pub and Cafe
❂ Popular pub in the old town, with salads and fresh fish on the menu.
506 Pandora St.; Tel: (250) 361-3310; Category 3

Wharfside Eatery
Large and somewhat rustic terrace restaurant on the Inner Harbour. The menu includes mainly fresh fish and pizza.
1208 Wharf St.; Tel: (250) 360-1808; Category 2

SHOPPING

Market Square
These beautifully renovated brick structures of the warehouses on the waterfront now house shops, art galleries and restaurants.
560 Johnson St.

HOTELS

Canterbury Inn
Good middle category hotel. About a ten minute drive from the city centre.
80 rooms; 310 Gorge Rd. E; Tel: (250) 382-2151; Fax: 382-3856; Category 2

Empress
The best and most traditional address in the city. The impressive country house hotel on the Inner Harbour has recently been renovated.
481 rooms; 721 Government St.; Tel: (250) 384-8111, Fax: 381-4334, Category 1

INFORMATION

Tourism Victoria
The information office is directly on the Inner Harbour and offers leaflets and city maps as well as a room booking service.
812 Wharf St.; Tel: (250) 953-2033; Fax: 382-6539

SURROUNDING AREA

Butchart Gardens   (100/C5)
★ There are flowers in bloom and trees in leaf nearly all year round in this 20 hectare (50 acre) botanical garden. The complex features an idyllic park and various theme gardens. The most beautiful part of the entire area is an old quarry planted for the first time in 1904.
Brentwood, about 20 km (12,5 mi) north of Victoria; in summer daily 9 am–10.30 pm; other times 9 am–4 pm; admission: $15.50

Fort Rodd Hill   (100/C5)
An excursion west through the large port area of Victoria takes you to this old protected fortification. A particularly impressive attraction is Fisgard Lighthouse, built in 1860, the oldest lighthouse on the West Coast of Canada.
15 km (9 miles) west of Victoria, Hwy. 1A; daily 10 am–5.30 pm; admission: $3

Between the Rockies and the Pacific

Magnificent mountains, beautiful lakes, colourful pioneer towns: British Columbia has got it all

With no show of modesty at all, British Columbia — generally referred to as B.C. — calls itself the most beautiful province in Canada. And that appears to be a true statement. This Western region has the greatest diversity of scenery and offers the best possibilities for an adventure holiday in Canada. You fancy canoeing? Bowron Lakes are ideal. Looking at mountains? A trip through the magnificent Columbia Mountains in Glacier National Park will give every mountain fan something to marvel at. Skiing? The hi-tech lifts and slopes on Whistler will thrill every mountain skier and deep snow fans from all over the world come to the Monashee and Cariboo Mountains every winter to make their winter dreams of heli-skiing come true.

The list of opportunities is endless. Whether you're into fishing (salmon) or hiking, cycling or rafting, British Columbia has something for everyone. The province can even boast sunny beaches

On Yellowhead Highway

and warm waters as in the lakes of the Okanagan Valley.

The mainland of this just 950,000 sq km (370,000 sq mi) large province — Vancouver Island and the city of Vancouver in the extreme southwest deserve their own chapters — is a wide area to cover. The region is dominated by large mountain ranges — not only the Rockies, for these only begin at the extreme eastern edge of the province. Many other large mountain ranges — all part of the North American Cordilleras — run through the country in a north-south direction. The almost undeveloped Coast Mountains, which run along the tattered Pacific coast, reach heights of over 4,600 m (15,000 ft) — higher than the Rockies.

A journey through British Columbia is a constant up and down: green mountain ranges give way to remote high plateaus, into which rivers like the Fraser have cut wide valleys. Only the extreme northeast, the area around Dawson Creek, is flat. There the province reaches beyond the Rockies into the foothills of the prairies. The mountains therefore determine the vegetation and the climate in B.C.: The western slopes of the mountain ranges are rainy and thickly wooded, while in the plateaus to the east of the mountains the weather is almost always sunny and dry, allowing only pinewoods and grassy steppes to flourish. Southern B.C., protected by the mountains, has a surprisingly mild climate. At Osoyoos, on the US border, you will find the only desert in Western Canada – complete with cacti and rattlesnakes.

CARIBOU REGION

(**100/C2-3**) The steppe-like high plateau on the upper reaches of the Fraser River is the Wild West of Canada: hilly ranch country with large herds of cattle, abandoned gold rush towns up country. The Caribou Waggon Road was built to serve the mountain dwellers in the first gold rush of 1860, and it was the first road in Western Canada. Highway 97 now follows the old route from the South and provides access to the region. Even today, many of the small ranch villages, which generally grew from mail coach stations, are named after their distance from the beginning of the road at *Lillooet* (**100/C4**): 70 Mile House, 100 Mile House etc.

As you drive along Caribou Highway, you keep coming across lakes with sandy shores which make you want to take a swim. The main centre and starting point for tours up country is *Williams Lake* (**100/C3**), where a rodeo is held every year on 1 July. Up country in the remote Caribou Mountains you will find the best-known ghost town in the region, *Barkerville, as well as* a number of other abandoned gold rush towns still waiting to be discovered, like *Likely* or *Horsefly*. If you want to go even further into the wilderness, you should take a trip along Hwy. 20, which runs west from William's Lake through *Tweedsmuir Provincial Park* to the coast at *Bella Coola* (ferry connection to Port Hardy)

MARCO POLO SELECTION: BRITISH COLUMBIA

1 Flower meadows on Mount Revelstoke
Alpine colours, but only in high summer (page 54)

2 Fort St. James
A look at the life of the fur traders of yesteryear (page 59)

3 Hayes Point Provincial Park
The most beautiful bathing area (page 55)

4 Helmcken Falls
Rushing whitewater – very photogenic (page 57)

5 Nakusp Hot Springs
Hot springs and wonderful green nature (page 54)

6 Purcell Lodge
Modern wilderness lodge in a spectacular location (page 52)

— near to where Alexander Mackenzie reached the Pacific in 1792 after crossing Canada for the very first time.

SIGHTSEEING

Barkerville   (100/C2)
At the time of the gold rush of 1870, Barkerville was the biggest city north of San Francisco — a boomtown full of adventurers, loose women and hopeful Gold Diggers. All that remains is a wonderfully nostalgic historic site with dilapidated Western facades, boardwalk pavements and actors re-enacting the pioneer era.
Visitor Centre with museum at the entrance to the site. On Hwy. 26, daily 8 am to dusk; admission in summer: $5.50

Cottonwood House   (100/C2)
A sympathetically restored mail coach station dating back to 1864. Coach rides.
On Hwy. 26; daily 10 am–4 pm; admission: $2

ACCOMMODATION

There are lots of cheap motels and campsites on Highway 97. A stay in a lodge or on a ranch is also recommended. Some examples:

Becker's Lodge
Equipment and canoe rental for the approximately one week canoe trip on Bowron Lakes.
10 rooms; Box 129; Wells, B.C. V0K 2R0; Tel: (250) 992-8864; Fax: 992-8893; Category 2–3

Bracewell's Alpine Wilderness
Comfortable, isolated wilderness lodge (riding, hiking, fishing).

11 rooms and log cabins; Box 1, Tatlayoko Lake, B.C. V0L 1W0; Tel:: and Fax: (250) 476-1169; Category 1

Springhouse Trails Ranch
Well-kept holiday ranch run by Germans. Campsite.
20 rooms; P.O. Box 2; RR 1, Williams Lake, B.C. V2G 2P1; Tel: (250) 392-4780; Category 2

INFORMATION

Caribou Tourism Association
P.O. Box 4900; Williams Lake, B.C. V2G 2V8; Tel: (250) 392-2226; Fax: 392-2838

DAWSON CREEK

(103/F3) Dawson Creek (11,000 pop.) would be an insignificant farming town, were it not for 'Milestone 0' on the main street in the centre of town. This is where the famous *Alaska Highway*, begins, which runs almost 2,300 km (1,500 mi) all the way to Delta Junction in Alaska. Exhibitions in the *Visitor Center* and the *Walter Wright Pioneer Village* illustrate the history of the region and the story of the Alaska Highway.

SURROUNDING AREA

Muncho Lake   (103/D1)
The emerald green 11 km (7 mi) long lake about 700 km (440 mi) north of Dawson Creek is in one of the most beautiful areas anywhere on the Alaska Highway. You can wash away the dust from the wilderness at *Liard Hot Springs. Highland Glen Lodge (40 rooms, 10 cabins, at milestone 462; Tel: (250) 776-3481; Fax: 776-3482; Category 1–2)* offers good accommodation

The famous Alaska Highway starts in Dawson Creek

on the lakeside and excursions in the area, for example in *Nahanni National Park.*

GLACIER NATIONAL PARK

(104/A–B5) Lots of black and grizzly bears live in the 1350 sq km (520 sq mi) protected area in he glacier covered Selkirk Mountains, up which Highway 1 makes its arduous climb. At a height of 1327 m (4380 ft), at ◆❱❱ *Rogers Pass*, there is a memorial to the completion of the Trans-Canada Highway in 1962. In the *Visitor Centre* nextdoor the park wardens can give you tips for your hiking tours. Watch out: it rains a lot along the west side of the mountains!

The exhibitions in the small *museum* at the Visitor Centre illustrate how difficult it must have been to build this road a good 100 years ago. Accommodation and restaurants are available in the old railway town of *Golden* (4000 pop.) at the eastern entrance to the Park.

HOTELS

Columbia Valley Lodge
Quiet guest-house south of Golden. Good starting point for tours in the nearby National Parks.
12 rooms; P. O. Box 2669; Golden, B.C. V0A 1H0; Tel/Fax: (250) 348-2508; Category 3

Purcell Lodge
★ Comfortable and magnificently situation lodge above the tree-line. Can only be reached on foot or by helicopter.
10 rooms, incl. full board; P. O. Box 1829, Golden, B.C. V0A 1H0; Tel: (250) 344-2639; Fax: 344-5520; Category 1

KAMLOOPS

(101/D 4) When travelling in B.C., you will come to Kamloops. Not because the third biggest city (75,000 pop.) in the province is particularly impressive, but because it is at the intersection of the main Highways and, with its big shopping malls, it is a good supply point for trips up country.

The city centre, with *Victoria Street as* the main shopping street, runs along the southern bank of the Thompson River.

MUSEUM

Secwepemc Native Heritage Center

Exhibitions and a reconstructed village illustrate the culture of the Shuswap Indians. Dance and music displays.

355 Yellowhead Hwy.; in summer daily 9 am–8 pm; other times 9 am–5pm; admission: $6

RESTAURANT

Sinbad's Restaurant

Pleasant venue. River terrace. Steaks, fish.

1502 River St.; Tel: (250) 372-1522; Category 2

HOTELS

Ramada

Reliable and respectable middle category hotel on the hill above the city. Restaurant, pool.

114 rooms; 555 West Columbia St.; Tel: (250) 374-0358; Fax: 374-0691; Category 2

Riverland Motel

Plain, clean motel on the river, away from the bustle of the Trans-Canada Highway.

58 rooms; 1530 River St.; Tel: (250) 374-1530; Fax: 374-1534, Category 3

SURROUNDING AREA

Adams River   (101 / D 4)

The salmon come upstream to spawn everywhere along the West Coast. The most spectacular *salmon run* takes place at the beginning of October in the Adams River, just 70 km (44 mi) south of Kamloops. Several hundred thousand bright red sockeye salmons jostle in the knee-deep water. Every four years there is a bumper year: within two weeks more than a million salmon come to spawn and die — the next time will be in 2002.

Shuswap Lakes   (101/D4)

The big lake area east of Kamloops is a popular area for *water sports fans.* Shuswap Lake alone has more than 1,000 km (625 mi) of shoreline — densely wooded and barely occupied. In the small towns like Salmon Arm or Sicamous you can rent houseboats and explore the labyrinth of branches and inlets on the lakes at your leisure.

LYTTON

(101/D4) The tiny village (400 pop.), located where the Thompson River flows into the Fraser River, is a popular base for *whitewater rafting.* Just to the south is the start of the impressive ☙ Fraser River canyon, in which the river makes its way for a good 100 km (62 mi) through the Coast Mountains. At *Hell's Gate,* the narrowest point of the canyon, around 50 km (30 mi) south of Lytton, a ☙ *cablecar* goes down 150 m (500 ft) to the riverbank where you can watch salmon struggle upstream in the fish ladders in summer.

SPORTS

Kumsheen Raft Adventures

Rafting on the Thompson and Fraser Rivers.

Lytton, 281 Main St.; Tel: (604) 455-2296

Ashcroft   (101/D4)
During the gold rush era, Ashcroft was a flourishing town, but since the modern Highway left it behind, the 1700 inhabitant village about 70 km (44 mi) north of Lytton has been dreaming of better times. *Ashcroft Manor,* an old roadhouse, and the *Ashcroft Museum (404 Brink St.)* tell you all about the good old days.

MT. REVELSTOKE NATIONAL PARK

(101/E3) From July until the beginning of September the ★ mountain meadows at the top of Mt. Revelstoke flourish — an unforgettable experience. Over a hundred species of wild flower grow here. Access is easy: a gravel road runs up the 1938 m (6400 ft) high mountain (in high summer there is a shuttlebus). At the top you will find some wonderful ❧ short trails, ideal for a half day trip. Below in the valley, it's worth taking a walk along the *Giant Cedars Trail,* an educational trail which runs from the Trans-Canada Highway through the thick ancient forest with centuries-old cedars and Douglas firs. There are restaurants, hotels and campsites in Revelstoke (8000 pop.) at the foot of the mountain.

TOURS

Selkirk Mountain Experience
A several day long hike in the wilderness to the glaciers in the Selkirk Mountains. Accommodation in a mountain hut. Advance booking is required:
P. O. Box 2998; Revelstoke, B.C. V0E 2S0; Tel: (250) 837-2381; Fax: 837-4685

HOTELS

Regent Inn
Stylish and historic hotel in the centre of town with a good restaurant.
45 rooms, Revelstoke, 112 1st St. E, Tel: (250) 837-2107, Fax: 837-9669, Category 2

SURROUNDING AREA

Arrow Lakes   (101/E4)
Revelstoke is at the north end of a long string of lakes on the Columbia River. You can explore the largely undeveloped region on Highways 23 und 6 and discover historic towns such as *Kaslo* as well as hot springs like the ★ *Nakusp Hot Springs* and ghost towns like *Sandon. Car ferries* cross at lots of places.

Revelstoke Dam
Visitor Centre   (101/E4)
The ultra-modern visitor centre at the north entrance to the site explains the function of an embankment type dam on the Columbia River. If you're interested in technology, carry on to the enormous *Mica Dam* about 150 km (94 mi) upstream and take the tour there.

OKANAGAN VALLEY

(101/D4) This valley, formed by a long chain of lakes, has become an orchard and wine-growing area as well as a very popular

The meadows around Mt. Revelstoke are in bloom all summer

holiday centre of Western Canada on account of its dry and sunny climate. The southern end of the valley so dry that even cacti grow there. In spring, when the apple, cherry and peach trees are in blossom on the plantations, the slopes around the lakes shine with colour. In summer and autumn you can buy *regional produce* from lots of street stalls: honey, jam, ciders and, of course, all kinds of fresh fruit. It's worth stopping at any of the *wineries* you will come across all over the valley, many of which have some good wines to offer.

The main town in the valley is *Kelowna* on the Eastern shore of Okanagan Lake, approx. 150 km (94 mi) long. In recent years the town has grown to around 90,000 inhabitants — many of them pensioners who pass their days here in the sun playing golf and tennis. Lovely bathing beaches, as for example in the ★ *Hayes Point Provincial Park*, mainly in the southern part of the valley near *Osoyoos* and *Penticton*, where a big peach festival is held at the end of July. The many water parks with their huge slides are particularly exciting for children.

SIGHTSEEING

Gray Monk Cellars

Everything you have ever wanted to know about Canadian viticulture. Hourly tours followed by wine-tastings with wonderful ❧ views over the lake.
Camp Rd., Okanagan Centre, 20 km north of Kelowna; daily 11 am–4 pm; admission free

O'Keefe Ranch
The ranch, which was established in 1867, is now an open-air museum, which gives an insight into the lives of the early pioneers.
9 km (6 miles) north of Vernon on Hwy. 97; in summer daily 9 am–5 pm; admission $ 6

RESTAURANTS

Earl's on Top Restaurant
Fish, steak und pasta on the lakeside. Terrace on upper floor.
Kelowna, 211 Bernard Av.; Tel: (250) 763-2777; Category 2

Salty's Beach House
✱ Fish restaurant on the beach.
Penticton, 988 Lakeshore Dr.; Tel: (250) 493-5001; Category 2

HOTELS

Bel Air Motel
Simple motel near Skaha Lake with pool and launderette.
42 rooms; Penticton, 2670 Skaha Lake Rd.; Tel: (250) 492-6111, Fax: 492-8035; Category 3

Eldorado
Small but stylish hotel with views over the lake. Restaurant on the verandah.
20 rooms; Kelowna, Pandosy St./ Cook Rd.; Tel: (250) 763-7500; Fax: 861-4779; Category 1–2

Siesta Motor Inn
Pleasant motel with small apartments not far from the lake.
96 rooms, Kelowna, 3152 Lakeshore Rd.; Tel: (250) 763-5013; Fax: 763-1265; Category 2

INFORMATION

Thompson Okanagan Tourism Association
1332 Water Street, Kelowna, B.C. V1Y 9P4; Tel: (250) 860-5999; Fax: 860-9993

QUEEN CHARLOTTE ISLANDS

(**102/B 4-5**) The rainy, frequently storm-battered archipelago, formerly the home of the Haida In-

---

Inventive Canadians

Canada has definitely made its contribution towards supplying the world with new ideas and discoveries. Alexander Graham Bell invented the telephone, Eddie Ezra Butler the match and the Swedish immigrant Gideon Sundback the zip fastener. The two doctors, Frederick Banting and Charles Best discovered insulin in 1929 at the University of Toronto. And in 1879 the railway engineer, Stanford Fleming, proposed an idea truly novel to everyone of dividing the world into 24 time zones.

And there are also a whole series of 'typically Canadian' inventions to help Canadians in their own country, for example, the snowmobile, the snow propeller and the combine harvester which revolutionised farming in the prairies. And there are even more wonderful inventions without which life would not be worth living: like the paint roller or instant mashed potato!

dians, is a vertiable "Galapagos of the North" with rain forests, sea lions, bald eagles and a wide range of sea creatures.

The *Museum* in Queen Charlotte City (950 pop., ferry from Prince Rupert) on Graham Island in the north documents the ancient culture of the Haida who once hunted whales from their canoes *(May–Sept daily 9 am–5 pm; all other times 1 pm –5 pm).*

You can still see *totem poles* in some old villages on the island. A large part of Moresby Island in the south and its unique ecosystem have been protected in *Gwaii Haanas National Park.*

TOURS

Ecosummer Expeditions
Kayak trips along the coast of the Queen Charlotte Islands.
1516 Duranleau St., Vancouver, B.C. V6H 3S4; Tel: (604) 669-7741; Fax: 669 321

Maple Leaf Adventures
Five to eleven day boat and kayak trips along the West Coast.
19-2625 Muir Rd., Courtenay, B.C. V9N 8S6; Tel: (250) 240-2420

WELLS GRAY PROVINCIAL PARK

(101/D3) The densely wooded, easily 5,000 sq km (1,900 sq mi) protected area at the northern edge of the Columbia Mountains is quite amous for its waterfalls, including the 137 m (450 ft) high ★ *Helmcken Falls* foaming down into a narrow valley framed with green. Almost as spectacular, near the Park entrance, is *Spahats Creek* with a 120 m (400 ft) deep canyon.

Fans of hiking in the wilderness can continue up country on the extensive trail network. The lake chain of Clearwater and Azure Lake is particularly suitable for canoeing. *Canoe rental* and accommodation are available at the Park entrance and also in Clearwater.

TOURS

Kanata Wilderness Adventures
Canoe and walking tours in the Park. Accommodation in a rustic guest ranch.
P.O. Box 1766, RR1, Clearwater, B.C. V0E 1N0; Tel: (250) 674-2774; Fax: 674-2197

WHISTLER

(100/C4) This beautifully kept and well set-out mountain village lies on the snowy Coast Mountains, about two hours' drive north of Vancouver. It has become a popular *holiday resort* in recent years. *Hiking, golf* and *mountain-biking* are the summer attractions.

In winter, *heli-skiing* and the ultra-modern *slopes* on both Whistler Mountain and Blackcomb Mountain — with ten high-speed four-chair lifts, 14 other lifts, two cablecars and a height difference of 1,200 m (4,000 ft) draw the visitors — a top-class ski resort.

Some of the lifts are also operating in summer, so that you can take a lofty ride up to the peaks to hike or bike. You may also enjoy some summer skiing high up on a glacier. Down below in the valley, life centres around the pedestrian zone of Whistler Village, where you find shops, restaurants and cafes all closely packed together.

Gaitors Bar & Grill

❖ You can try fiery Tex-Mex cuisine here.

At the Shoestring Lodge; Tel: (250) 938-5777; Category 2–3

Pika's

〰 This restaurant features a magnificent view over the Coast Mountains.

Located at the Whistler cablecar mountain station; Tel: (250) 932-3434; Category 2

HOTELS

Chateau Whistler

Elegant holiday hotel right by the lift valley station. Excellent golf course. Rates are relatively inexpensive in the summer.

563 rooms; Whistler Village; Tel: (250) 938-8000; Fax: 938-2055; Category 1

Durlacher Hof

Comfortable, first-class guest house with an Austrian feel.

8 rooms, 7055 Nesters Rd.; Tel: (250) 932-1924; Fax: 938-1980; Category 2

YELLOWHEAD REGION

(100–101/A1–D2) Yellowhead Highway 16, opened in 1970, is the second major east-west highway in Western Canada after the Trans-Canada Highway further south. It runs from the prairies through Edmonton and Jasper

A reconstructed Git'ksan village: 'Ksan Indian Village

58

across the lonely, wild North to the Pacific Coast, following the old trapper pack routes and giving access (with some off-shoots like the Cassiar Highway) to the far north of British Columbia. The road was named after a blonde trapper, and his 'yellow head' still appears on road signs today.

From the borders with Alberta in the Jasper National Park, the Highway crosses the deep forests of the Fraser Plateau. It's quite normal here for a black bear to wander across the road now and then. To the West of the felling town of *Prince George* (75,000 pop., **100/C2**) the road passes through a huge area of lakes to the Coast Mountains, where the territory of the Northwest Coast Indians begins.

At *Moricetown Canyon* on the Bulkley River you can watch salmon being caught in July and August in some places. Nearby, in the area around *Hazelton* (**100/B1**), lots of old *totem poles* in the reservation villages of the Tsimshian Indians display the great carving skills of the tribe.

Prince Rupert (17,000 pop., **100/A1–2**), at the Western end of Yellow-head Highway, is an important fishing, coal and grain port, providing a link to the West Coast ferry system: B.C. Ferries operate from here south to Vancouver Island, the ships of the Alaska Marine Highway provide transport on to Alaska (it is recommended to book both routes a few months in advance).

MUSEUMS

Fort St. James   (100/C2)
★ A journey into the past: the fur trading post set up by Simon

Fraser in 1806 has been restored and made into an excellent museum site with costumed trappers re-enacting the harsh daily life of 1896.
50 km (30 mi) north of Vanderhoof on Highway 27; in summer daily 9am–5pm; admission $4

'Ksan Indian Village   (100/B1)
A reconstruction of a Git'ksan Indian village with the almost obligatory totem poles and carving workshops. Dancing displays in summer.
Hazelton; daily 9 am–5pm; guided tours $7

TOURS

Spatzisi Wilderness Vacations
Walking, riding and rafting trips in the completely isolated mountain regions in the North of B.C. Advance booking essential.
P. O. Box 3070, Smithers, B.C. V0J 2N0; Tel: (250) 847-2909; Fax: 847-9039

INFORMATION

Northern BC Tourism Association
11–3167 Tatlow Rd., Smithers, B.C. V0J 2N0; Tel: (250) 847-5227; Fax: 847-4321

SURROUNDING AREA

Stewart   (100/A1)
From Kitwanga you can take the *Cassiar Highway* for a visit to the magnificent glaciered mountains on the border with Alaska. It is 240 km (150 mi) to Stewart at the end of a 145 km (91 mi) long fjord. Alaska starts in the agreeably run-down neighbouring village of *Hyder*, as you can easily tell, because the ☻ bars don't shut.

On the dream highway of the world

The Rocky Mountains are the home of the most — and the most beautiful — National Parks in Canada

Whether you're looking at a postcard or a picture book of Canada, it will most probably show a scene from the Rocky Mountains: a deep green glacier lake and jagged peaks, with colourful meadows of flowers or grizzlies eating bilberries.

The Rockies region has everything you think of as typical of Canada. So it's not surprising that the mountains on the border between Alberta and British Columbia are also the best known and most popular holiday region in the West. Five big National Parks attract visitors, four of which — Banff, Jasper, Kootenay and Yoho — border immediately onto each other to form a unique, easily 20,000 sq km (7,700 sq mi) nature protection area.

The finest of magnificent mountain scenery — but not regimented with huts and motorways as you see in the Alps. The

Indians came from the plains into the mountains only to hunt, and it has only been 200 years since the first white fur traders came to the region. To date only four passes go through the Canadian section of the Rockies, and only a few — very spectacular — highways give access to the region. In the Parks themselves, there is a very good network of trails, along which you can hike for a few hours, or even for a week or more, in complete solitude. The Canadian Rockies are still largely undeveloped. Certainly inside the Parks, but even outside the protected areas, you will only find some scattered small settlements and camps for hunters and anglers.

In high summer, however, the number of visitors to the Parks is enormous — fortunately only in the well-known places like Banff, Jasper and Lake Louise. The hotels there are generally booked up, and if you haven't booked you'll have great difficulty finding a bed for the night. It is very rewarding to take a

Lake O'Hara, a beautiful mountain lake in relatively undeveloped Yoho National Park

lodge up country for several days and use it as a base to take peaceful hikes in the side valleys.

But back to the mountains themselves: The Rockies are the eastern strand of the North American Cordilleras. They stretch from far south in New Mexico through the US states of Colorado, Wyoming and Montana to Canada. In Canada itself the mighty Rocky Mountains are still 1200 km (750 mi) long, extending all the way to the Yukon Territory. The mountain ranges are made up of sedimentary rock, slate, lime and sandstone, which were once deposited on the bottom of an ancient sea.

About 600 million years ago the mountains began to fold upwards – always the north-South mountain ranges, as the continental drift pushed the Pacific plate from the west against the North American mainland plate. The ice age glaciers later carved out valleys, leaving behind turquoise lakes of melt water and large moraines – a dream setting for the modern nature fan and wilderness lover.

BANFF NATIONAL PARK

(104/B5) In summer Banff Avenue and the well known glacier lake, Lake Louise, are bustling with tourists. Still, the oldest National Park in Canada is well worth the trip: 6,640 sq km (2,560 sq mi) of glacier valleys, emerald lakes and snow covered mountains around Bow River valley. Get hiking maps from the Park Wardens at the Visitor Centre at Banff or Lake Louise – away from the roads, on the more than 1,300 km (815 mi) of paths up-country, it soon gets much quieter.

In 1885, when the railway was built through the region, the Canadian government decided to protect the mountain area. It all

MARCO POLO SELECTION: ROCKY MOUNTAINS

1 Icefields Parkway
The most spectacular panoramic road in the Rockies (pages 63 and 66)

2 Jasper Park Lodge
Luxury in the wild – a well kept lodge (page 67)

3 Lake Louise
Despite the tourist bustle the most beautiful lake in the Rockies (page 63)

4 Mt. Assiniboine Lodge
A mecca for hikers – and, in winter, for cross-country skiers (page 65)

5 Takkakaw Falls
The highest waterfalls in the Rockies (page 71)

6 Waterton Shoreline Cruises
Boat trip in the mountains (page 70)

started with a dispute about ownership rights of the hot springs at Banff, and the government decided – wisely – that this unique landscape should remain unspoilt for future generations.

Thanks to the severe restrictions, only a small part of the Park has been developed over the years: the town of Banff (5,000 pop.) came into being, some – really quite good – ski resorts have been established, and on the peak of Sulphur Mountain there is a ❧ cablecar with a panoramic view over the town and Bow River. On Lake Louise, too, a few hotels have materialized out of the forest, but these oases of civilisation are still surrounded by wild mountains as they always have been.

SIGHTSEEING

Banff Springs Hotel

❧ The grand palace at the end of Spray Avenue in Banff was built by Canadian Pacific Railroad in 1886. The driving force behind the construction of the palatial hotel was the Railway Director, William Van Horne. In keeping with his motto, "If we can't export the scenery, we'll have to import the tourists", he had a series of luxury hotels built along the Trans-Canadian Railway, which had been completed in 1885.

The Banff Springs is one of the most beautiful examples of these "Railway Hotels". Marilyn Monroe stayed here when she was filming "River of no Return".

Icefields Parkway

★ The "dream highway of the Rockies" (Hwy. 93) runs for about 230 km (140 mi) from Lake Louise to Jasper, along the mountain ridge: an uninterrupted series of glaciers and mountain lakes, water falls and 3000 m (9,900 ft) high peaks.

It's worth getting there early as the best views are to the west, and the morning sun bathes the brightly polished rock faces and ice falls in delicate pink. Keep your camera at the ready, because you're likely to see one of the park's residents at the side of the road: an elk or moose, mountain sheep or mountain goat – and if you're lucky, even a grizzly. The most wonderful view awaits you at ❧ Bow Pass: from your 2,086 m (6,880 feet) vantage point the milky green Peyto Lake beckons you from the valley.

Lake Louise

★ The most famous mountain lake in Canada at the foot of the 3,464 m (11,400 ft) high Mt. Victoria gleams turquoise. On the shoreline promenade in front of Chateau Lake Louise (another "railway hotel") there is always a big crowd but on the paths round about it soon gets quieter. Make sure you allow half a day or a whole day for a hike, for example on the Big Beehive/Lake Agnes Trail or the Plain of Six Glaciers Trail.

MUSEUMS

Cave and Basin Centre

Exhibitions on Park history in the old bath house for the hot springs, to which the Park owes its existence.

Banff, Cave Av., July/Aug daily 9 am–6 pm; other times 9.30 am–5 pm; admission $2.25

Luxton Museum

Life-size figures and dioramas illustrate the way of life of the Blackfoot and Sarcee Indians: particularly interesting for children (good museum shop).

Banff, 1 Birch Av., daily 10 am–6 pm; in summer until 9 pm; admission $6

Natural History Museum

Exhibitions on the natural history and the animal and plant world of the Rockies.

Banff, 112 Banff Av.; July/Aug daily 10 am–8 pm; other times 10 am–6 pm; admission free

RESTAURANTS

Barbary Coast

Pizza and pasta, crisp salads and steaks.

Banff, 119 Banff Av.; Tel: (403) 762-4616; Category 2

Ristorante Classico

Elegant evening restaurant in the Rimrock Hotel. Excellent Italian cuisine and a great ☼ view of the mountains.

Banff, Sulphur Mountain Rd.; Tel: (403) 762-1840; Category 1

The Keg

Thick steaks and fish served in a Western atmosphere. Also a large salad bar. The adjacent bar is very popular with the locals.

Banff, 521 Banff Av.; Tel: (403) 762-4442; Category 2

SPORTS

Canadian Mountain Holidays

Reliable heli-skiing tour organiser in the partially accessible mountains west of the National Park. Accommodation in luxurious lodges up country.

Postal address: P.O. Box 1660, Banff, AB T0L 0C0; Tel: (403) 762-7100; Fax: 762-5879

Explore Holidays

You can rent wilderness lodges here and also book guided tours through the Rockies, hikes and accompanied cycle rides on Icefields Parkway. Book in advance if you can!

Postal address: P.O. Box 1709, Cochrane, AB T0L 0W0; Tel: (403) 932-7833; Fax: 932-7933

Park & Pedal

Bicycle rental in Banff for day trips in the area. Good tips for routes. *Banff, 229 Wolf St.; Tel: (403) 762-3191*

Timberline Tours

Horse-back rides by Bow Lake, several-day pack trips up country. *P.O. Box 14, Lake Louise, AB T0L 1E0; Tel: (403) 522-3743*

Upper Hot Springs

A hot bath to relax your muscles after walking.

Banff, Mountain Av.; in summer daily 10 am–11 pm; admission $7

Hiking

Right on the edges of Banff there are some shorter paths like the Fenland Trail (1.5 km/1 mile educational trail) to the Vermillion Lakes area. Despite their proximity to the Trans-Canada Highway, you will often see elks, moose and beavers here. From the Mount-Norquay ski resort car park a good 2 km (1.3 mi) long trail climbs up to the peak of ☼ Stoney Squaw Mountain and a breathtaking view over Banff Valley and Lake Minnewanka. Other good hiking areas for days

---

'Howdy, pardner!'

Canadians are a friendly people. Visitors from abroad will often hear them greet one another with 'Hi' and 'Howdy', whether it's on a hiking trail, at the nearby table at a locale or at a camping place — and the further you are from a large city, the more often you'll hear these words of welcome. Don't be surprised if someone you've just met addresses you by your first name: In nearly all situations, an acquaintanceship will be concluded with first names. That's not to be taken as tactless familiarity, but simply as the national custom.

---

out are the Spray River valley, Sunshine Meadows and the Johnstone Canyon. Also highly recommended are the trails which start at Lake Louise and nearby at Moraine Lake or over the Sentinel Pass to Paradise Valley or to Wenkchemna Pass.

HOTELS

You should book your accommodation a few months in advance if possible for high summer.

Banff Caribou Lodge

Well-kept, new hotel at the top of the middle category range. Particularly pleasant because of its location in the centre.
200 rms., Banff, 521 Banff Av.; Tel: (403) 762-5887; Fax: 762-5918; Category 2

Bow View Motor Lodge

Quiet hotel on the river bank only a short walk from Banff's main street.
57 rooms; 228 Bow Av.; Tel: (403) 762-2261; Fax: 762-8093; Category 2

Deer Lodge

Small, rustic hotel only a few minutes by foot from Lake Louise.

73 rooms, P. O. Box 100, Lake Louise; Tel: (403) 522-3747; Fax: 522-3883; Category 1–2

Mt. Assiniboine Lodge

★ Extremely cosy, rustic lodge dating back to 1928, complete-ly isolated in a high valley at the southern edge of Banff National Park. Idyllic position at the foot of Mount Assiniboine, the "Matterhorn of the Rockies". Only accessible on foot or by helicopter.
6 rooms, 6 cabins; Postal address: P. O. Box 1527, Canmore, AB T0L 0M0; Tel: (403) 678-2883; Fax: 678-4877; Category 2

Num-Ti-Jah Lodge

Very simple, historical lodge on Bow Lake, run by an interesting old-timer. Good base for hiking and horse-back riding.
24 rooms; P. O. Box 39, Lake Louise; Tel: (403) 522-2167; Fax: 522-2425; Category 2

Post Hotel

Stylish mountain hotel with "original" Austrian alpine charm and an excellent restaurant. Many of the 100 rooms have open fires.
P. O. Box 69, Lake Louise; Tel: (403) 522-3989; Fax: 522-3966, Category 1

Banff National Park

Maps and information on campsites, hiking routes, trekking tours etc.: *Tel: (403) 762-1550, Fax: 762-3229; Postal address: P. O. Box 900, Banff, AB T0L 0C0*

There are visitor centres on Highway 1 in Lake Louise and in Banff: *224 Banff Av., both daily 8 am–8 pm; in winter 9 am–5 pm*

CROWSNEST PASS

(**104/B6**) Crowsnest Pass is the southernmost pass through the Canadian Rockies. It was once an important Indian trade route. Now the modern Highway 3 crosses the thickly wooded mountains here at 1,396 metres (4,610 ft). The town of Crowsnest Pass really only comprises a series of small settlements like Bellevue, Frank and Coleman, which stretch out along the Highway. They all came into being around the turn of the century as mining towns, as the region is rich in coal seams. Frank earned tragic fame in 1903 when a landslide buried the settlement and claimed 60 dead. An excellent museum on the still identifiable site of the *Frank Slide* displays the pioneer history of the region.

Frank Slide Interpretive Centre, May–Sept daily 9 am–8 pm; at other times 10 am–4 pm; admission: $4

JASPER NATIONAL PARK

(**104/A–B4**) The great sight of the gleaming white Athabasca glacier, almost reaching the road on ★ *Icefields Parkway* is a highlight of any tour of the Rockies. The glacier tongue is part of the 325 sq km (126 sq mi) Columbia Icefield, a relic of the last Ice Age, emptying its meltwater into three oceans: the Atlantic, the Pacific and the Arctic Ocean.

Only 100 years ago the ice filled the entire valley, through which Highway 93 now runs. Signs at the side of the road show by the years, how quickly the glacier receded. The glacier tours available on special vehicles are for the less active tourists but a guided *Glacier Walk* on the ice should not be missed *(Start at the Visitor Centre on Hwy. 93; Tel: (403) 852-6550).*

But there is even more to see in this extremely wild Park: the raging *Athabasca Falls* on Icefields Parkway and the idyllic ↘↗ *Maligne Lake* or a relaxing *bath in the hot springs* of Miette. Accommodation, campsites and restaurants are available in the only town in the Park, *Jasper.*

Jasper Tramway

Cablecar on ↘↗ Whistlers Mountain to a wonderful panoramic view across the valley from Jasper. Paths around the mountain peak.

Whistler Rd., in the summer 8.30 am–10 pm daily; in the spring and autumn: 9.30 am–5 pm; fare $14

Maligne Lake Boat Tours

This company offers one and a half hour tours of the biggest glacier lake in the Rockies with its much photographed Spirit Island. Late afternoon is the best time for the tour.

In summer daily, every hour, 10 am–5 pm; bookings in Jasper, 626 Connaught Dr.; Tel: (403) 852-3370, fare $31

RESTAURANT

Papa George's
Restaurant with bar in the Astoria Hotel. Steaks and fish dishes. *404 Connaught Dr.; Tel: (403) 852-3351, Category 2*

HOTELS

Alpine Village
Well-kept log cabins in the Athabasca River valley. Very comfortable with open fires.
41 rooms, Jasper, P.O. Box 610; Tel: (403) 852-3285, no Fax, Category 1-2

Jasper Park Lodge
★ This is the luxury version of a log cabin in the wilderness: a well-kept holiday hotel in extensive grounds complete with its own private lake at the edge of Jasper. The lodge offers rooms in the main building as well as cozy old log cabins with open fireplace on the lakeside. Pretty busy in high summer, otherwise very comfortable and quiet. 18 hole golf course and four tennis courts.
442 rooms, Jasper, P.O. Box 40; Tel: (403) 852-3301; Fax: 852-507, Category 1

The romance of adventure with all comforts: Jasper Park Lodge

Tekarra Lodge

Rustic log cabins with open fires at the edge of Jasper. Good restaurant.

42 rooms; Jasper, P. O. Box 699; Tel: (403) 852-3058; Fax: 852-4636; Category 2

Freewheel Cycle

Bicycle rental for day excursions in Jasper National Park.
Jasper, 611 Patricia St.; Tel: (403) 852-3898

Maligne River Adventures

Rafting on the Maligne River as well as the (pleasantly less difficult) Athabasca River.
Jasper, 626 Connaught Dr., Tel: (403) 852-3370, Fax: 852-3405, Postal address: P. O. Box 280, Jasper, AB T0E 1E0

Skyline Trail Rides

Offers include three- or four-day riding trips which will take you into isolated side valleys in the Park with overnight accommodation in wilderness camps.
Advance bookings: P. O. Box 207, Jasper, Tel: (403) 852-4215, Fax: 865-1866

Hikes

Some of the most beautiful and most popular trails for short, none too strenuous hikes are to be found at the foot of Mount Edith Cavell and in Maligne Canyon, which is only a few metres across but up to 50 m (165 feet) deep.

The Tonquin Valley and the wilderness region surrounding Brazeau Lake are particularly suitable for both day hikes and longer trips.

Jasper National Park

The visitor centre is opposite the station on the main street.
Postal address: P. O. Box 10, Jasper, AB T0E 1E0; Tel: (403) 852-6161; Fax: 852-6152

Mt. Robson Provincial Park   (104/A4)

In this park, which adjoins Jasper to the west, is the highest peak in the Rocky Mountains, Mount Robson with a height of 3,954 m or 13,050 ft. Recommended: a one or two day hike along the Robson River at the foot of the ice-covered mountain to Berg Lake.

KIMBERLEY

(104/B6) "Upper Bavaria" is how this little town on the western edge of the Rocky Mountains describes itself. When the local mine closed in 1972 and the town threatened to become a ghost town, the city fathers decided to make their town into a Bavarian village. The surrounding mountain scenery is just right and the architecture is now quite alpine. In the small square on the main street is a larger than life cuckoo clock, the shops sell Bavarian knick-knacks and the musicians yodel in the restaurants. Even the hydrants here have had leather shorts painted on them — completely crazy.

More Canadian and of more historic interest is the very impressive *Museum village of Fort Steele*, about 30 km (19 mi) to the east, where life in a pioneer

In Kimberley even the hydrants have a "Bavarian" look

town in the gold rush era of the 1890's is displayed in more than 60 buildings. Of interest to children: a ride in an old mailcoach.

RESTAURANT

Old Bauernhaus
Snacks and beer in an original Bavarian building.
280 Norton Av.; Tel: (250) 427-5133; Category 3

SPORTS

Top of the World Ranch
Rustic, very comfortable guest ranch. Here, you can enjoy horse-back riding in a magnificent mountain setting.
10 rooms, 20 cabins, P.O. Box 29, Fort Steele, B.C. V0B 1N0; Tel: (250) 426-6306; Fax: 426-6377; Category 1

INFORMATION

Rocky Mountain Visitor Association
Information on accommodation, ranches, golf courses and hiking routes in the region.
350 Ross St.; Postal address: P.O. Box 10, Kimberley, B.C. V1A 2Y5; Tel: (250) 427-4838; Fax: 427-3344

KOOTENAY NATIONAL PARK

(104/B5) The still largely inaccessible, 1,406 sq km (540 sq mi) protected area around the Kootenay Valley is particularly good for several-day *hiking tours up country.* Starting on Highway 93, which crosses the Park, are some shorter trails, along *Marble Canyon* and to the bright orange and ochre *Paint Pots,* from which the Indians took their warpaint.

At the Southern entrance to the Park the up to 47 °C (117 °F) *Radium Hot Springs* bubble in a large pool. Restaurants and accommodation are available in the nearby small village of the same name.

HOTELS

Chalot
Well-kept guest house in alpine style. Wonderful ☁️ view over the valley.
17 rooms, P.O. Box 456, Radium, B.C. V0A 1M0; Tel: (250) 347-9305; Fax: 250-9306; Category 2

Radium Golf Resort
Modern holiday hotel with lots of sports facilities and two really good 18 hole golf courses.
119 rooms; P.O. Box 310, Radium, B.C. V0A 1M0; Tel: (250) 347-9311; Fax: 347-6299; Category 1–2

WATERTON LAKES NATIONAL PARK

(104/C6) This only 525 sq km (203 sq miles) Park on the edge of the Prairies was named after the long series of *mountain lakes* which stretch far over the border into the Glacier National Park in Montana, USA. Good *trails* lead into totally undeveloped country. The most beautiful short route is the trail in *Red Rock Canyon,* the fiery red walls of which are made from 1.5 billion years old sedimentary rock.

Cameron Lake has facilities for boat and canoe rental and in an enclosure at the northern edge of the Park there is a *herd of bison.* The best view across the lake and mountains is from the ◄▶ terrace of the *Prince of Wales Hotel* at the northern edge of Waterton Park, the only village in the protected area.

TOURS

Waterton Shoreline Cruises

★ ◄▶ Boat trips on Upper Waterton Lake. The southernmost point of the trip is in Gla-

The 384 m (1270 ft) high Takkakaw waterfalls in Yoho National Park

cier National Park in Montana, USA. The view of the jagged mountains is particularly good early in the morning. Also a ferry service for hikers to the trails in the southern part of the park.

Departures from Waterton Marina, in summer daily at 9 am, 10 am, 1 pm, 4 pm and 7 pm; Tel: (403) 859-2362, fare $18

HOTELS

Aspen Village Inn

Quiet motel in the centre of Waterton, set back from the main road.

50 rooms; Waterton Park; Tel: (403) 859-2255; Fax: 859-2033; Category 2

Kilmorey Lodge

Small, stylish and rustic hotel, directly on the lakeside. Good restaurant in the hotel.

23 rooms, Waterton, 117 Evergreen Av.; Tel: (403) 859-2334; Fax: 859-2342; Category 2

YOHO NATIONAL PARK

(104/B5) The "only" 1313 sq km (507 sq mi) Park around the Kicking Horse and Yoho River valleys on the west side of the Rocky Mountains is much less well known than its bigger neighbour, Banff National Park. As a result it is much quieter on the trails. But the mountain scenery is no less spectacular. The Park can be explored in a day long excursion from Lake Louise or Banff.

Particularly impressive are the 384 m (1270 ft) high ★ *Takkakaw waterfalls* — the second highest in

Canada — in the Wapta Icefield and the turquoise 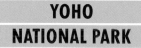 *Emerald Lake,* around which there is a very beautiful circular walk. The Trans-Canada Highway passes through the Park and climbs up *Kicking Horse Pass* (1647 m/5435 ft) across the Continental Divide. To overcome the grade, the railway engineers drilled two spiral tunnels in the mountain. You may see goods trains with more than 100 cars, the locomotive already coming out of the upper end of a tunnel while the rear cars are still going in.

HOTELS

Emerald Lake Lodge

Very well-kept holiday hotel with a good restaurant in a quiet location. Rooms in big log cabins on the shore of Emerald Lake.

85 rooms, P.O. Box 10, Field; Tel: (250) 343-6321; Fax: (403) 609-6158; Category 1

Kicking Horse Lodge

Simple, clean motel in Field, the only town in the Park. Central location but near the railway line. Small restaurant in the hotel.

14 rooms, Field, 100 Centre St.; Tel: (250) 343-6303; Fax: 343-6355; Category 2

INFORMATION/TOURS

Yoho Visitor Center

Joint Park and B.C. province visitor centre with small museum. The Park Wardens give guided tours once a week to the fossils in Burgess Shale, which are otherwise only accessible to scientists.

Field, Hwy. 1; Tel: (250) 343-6783, Fax: 343-60 12

Country of wheat and forests

The wide prairies of Alberta –
oil reserves and dinosaurs

Of course the Rocky Mountains, with their glaciers and turquoise lakes, are the most spectacular and best known region in the province of Alberta. The most beautiful part of the entire mountain range, which stretches from the USA into Yukon Territory, even lies in Alberta. But you shouldn't forget the other enormous part of the province, for the Rockies, at the southernmost western border, form only a small part of the 661,000 sq km (255,200 sq mi) province – an area which is almost twice as big as Germany. East of the mountains under the mostly bright blue skies stretch the endless prairies of Central Canada, which give way in the north to an enormous sub-arctic forest area.

Alberta, which was named after one of Queen Victoria's daughters, when it was elevated to a province in 1905, is still a country of farmers and ranchers, despite all the tourism in the Rockies. Small, sleepy villages, in which nothing seems to have changed

for 50 years, lie widely scattered. People live on the land, cultivating wheat, growing vegetables in their gardens, driving the cattle across the pasture – often by motorbike or helicopter now – and hunting in autumn to get in supplies for winter. Many Ukranians settled here in the waves of immigration at the turn of the century, as did many Germans and Scandinavians.

The wide prairies in the southern half of the province form part of the bread basket of Central Canada. In the foothills of the mountains large herds of cattle graze – 40 percent of all steaks in Canada come from Alberta. You could spend your holiday week on one of the big ranches playing cowboy for a time. The thickly wooded north however is largely unpopulated, few Highways pass through the only slightly undulating land. Logging and hunting are the only sources of income in so many pioneer towns on the Peace or Athabasca Rivers.

But cowboy and trapper nostalgia doesn't dominate everywhere in the province. Alberta is also the country of the oil

Splendid dinosaurs: an Albertosaurus

MARCO POLO SELECTION: ALBERTA

1 Canada Olympic Park
Look back to the 1988 winter Olympiad
(page 75)

2 Cook County Saloon
All the country music you can take
(page 79)

3 Head-Smashed-In Buffalo Jump
Indian cultural history — fascinating presentation
(page 80)

4 Ranchman's Saloon
Steaks and country music — the Wild West lives on!
(page 76)

5 Royal Tyrrell Museum of Paleontology
Enormous dinosaurs in a perfect primeval setting
(page 77)

6 West Edmonton Mall
The biggest shopping centre in the world
(page 78)

worker and the high-tech energy company. In 1914 the first oil well spurted up in the Turner Valley near Calgary. In 1947 more big oil deposits were discovered near the provincial capital, Edmonton. Since then both the main cities of Alberta — with great rivalry between them — have experienced a boom and the oil rich province now supplies a good 80 percent of fossil fuel resources to the whole of Canada.

The Mesozoic era did not only leave the province with oil and coal. Many dinosaurs lived in the extensive marshes at the edge of a primaeval lake — their fossilised bones appear everywhere out of the sedimentary strata in the mouths of riversand canyons in southern Alberta. Alberta is considered to be the biggest dinosaur cemetery in the world — to the delight of all dinosaur fans, who can admire the most spectacular finds in the excellent Royal Tyrell Museum in Drumheller.

CALGARY

(104/C5) As you stroll through *Stephen Street Mall* the city, with easily 830,000 inhabitants, looks pretty cosmopolitan: skyscrapers, boutiques, street cafes, sculptures and sophisticated malls, like those in the new *Bankers Hall* — a proud Manhattan of the Prairie. Calgary claimed world fame in 1988, when the Winter Olympics were held here. The Chinook wind is also well known, blowing down from the Rocky Mountains in winter like a hair drier and melting away all the snow.

The history of Calgary began in 1875 with the establishment of a police post on Bow River to combat the illegal whisky trade. In 1883 the first train steamed down the Transcanada Railway through the Prairies. Already the first rancheswere appearing and Calgary was becoming the most important centre of the meat industry in Canada. The discovery of oil in 1914 in Turner Valley triggered the first oil boom in Canada – ever since, the oil industry and Calgary have been on the up and up.

Nonetheless the city nurtures its cowboy image and holds the *Calgary Stampede,* the biggest rodeo in the world, every year.

SIGHTSEEING

The best introduction to the city is the view from the 191 m (626 feet) high ✌ *Calgary Tower:* To the East are the Prairies, in the West the Rocky Mountains dominate. Back on the ground, stroll through the city centre to the *Devonian Gardens (7th Ave./3rd St.),* a pretty botanical garden on the roof of a shopping centre. A little way to the north on Centre Street is Calgary's small *Chinatown,* where the eye is drawn by the newly built *Chinese Cultural Centre (197 1st Street).*

To the east on the bank of the Bow River you can still see the foundations of the old police post *Fort Calgary,* and opposite, on an island in the river, is the large *Calgary Zoo,* where children in particular will be excited by the wonderful dinosaur replicas.

MUSEUMS

Canada Olympic Park
★ Everything you ever wanted to know about the Winter Olympics. You can even bobsleigh on the simulator.
On the western edge of the city, Hwy. 1, in summer daily 9 am–6 pm; in winter 10 am– 4 pm; admission: $3.75

Glenbow Museum
The history of the Indians and settlers in Western Canada, documented on three floors.
130 9th Av. SE, in summer daily 9 am-5 pm; in winter Tues–Fri 9 am–5 pm; admission $8

Heritage Park Historical Village
This open air museum on the shores of Glenmore Reservoir shows life in the 'Wild West' of Canada in a reconstructed pioneer village. Steamer and paddle steamer trips.
South of city centre, 1900 Heritage Dr. SW, in summer daily 9 am– 5 pm; in spring and autumn only open at weekends; admission: $10

RESTAURANTS

Buzzard's Cowboy Cuisine
Western flair in the middle of the city: a barbecue restaurant, original style, substantial cowboy food. Excellent ribs.
140 10th Av. SW, Tel: (403) 264-6959; Category 2

Caesar's
Good steaks, elegant, pleasant atmosphere.
512 4th Av. SW, Tel: (403) 264-1222; Category 1

Eau Claire Market
Several popular restaurants and bars draw the crowds to this shopping centre: e. g. the ★ *Hard Rock Café,* the fashionable *Joey Tomatoes* and the pool bar ❂ *The Garage.*

Mescalero
You can get fiery south-western and Latin-American food here. Hot music and good Margaritas in the bar.

1315 1st St. SW; Tel: (403) 266-3339; Category 2

Silver Dragon
Cantonese food in Chinatown, good Dim Sum.
106 3rd Av. SE; Tel: (403) 264-5326; Category 2

SHOPPING

Western clothing, stetsons and cowboy boots are without doubt the most popular souvenirs from Calgary. You'll find the best selection at *Alberta Boot (614 10th Av. SW)* and *Laemmle's Western Wear* in the Eaton Centre on *Stephen Avenue Mall,* where there are also other shopping centres. The newest shopping paradise is *Eau Claire Market* on the bank of Bow River.

HOTELS

Econolodge
Well-kept hotel chain, near the Trans-Canada Highway.
55 rooms, 2440 16th Av. NW; Tel: (403) 289-2561, Fax: 282-9713; Category 3

Highlander
Reliable middle-class hotel, only two stops from the city centre.
130 rooms, 1818 16th Av. NW; Tel:

(403) 289-1961; Fax: 289-3901; Category 2

Marriott Plaza
Luxurious. Opposite the Calgary Tower in the city centre.
384 rooms, 110 9th Av. SE; Tel: (403) 266-7331; Fax: 262-8442; Category 1

Westin Hotel Calgary
Large luxury hotel with the best location in the city centre.
525 rooms, 320 4th Av.; Tel: (403) 266-1611; Fax: 233-7471; Category 1

ENTERTAINMENT

There are bars and nightclubs on ♣ 11th Avenue SW between 4th and 8th Street, this particular section which is known as 'Electric Avenue' because of all the neon signs. Country & Western fans should go south to ★ *Ranchman's Saloon (9615 Macleod Trail S).* Closer to the city centre you'll find ☯ *Cowboys (9th Av./5th St. SW),* another popular Western saloon. Jazz fans should try *Kaos Cafe (718 17th Av.).*

INFORMATION

Visitor & Convention Bureau
237 8th Av. SE, Calgary, AB T2G 0K8; Tel: (403) 263-8510; Fax:

262-3809; info cinema in the Calgary Tower

SURROUNDING AREA

Drumheller (104/C5)
140 km (88 miles) northeast of Calgary are the Alberta Badlands, a peculiar area of erosion along the Red Deer River. Drive along the 54 km (32 mi) *Dinosaur Trail* and see the multi-coloured fluted gullies and strange rock pillars, where numerous fossils have come to light. The most impressive remains of the dinosaurs, which lived in this region 65 million years ago, can be seen in the ★ *Royal Tyrrell Museum of Paleontology.* Here the dawn of history is brought to life in a perfect setting. There is a Tyrannosaurus Rex as well as rare species of dinosaur with ducks' bills and webbed feet.
End May–beginning Sept daily 9 am–9 pm; other times Tues–Sun 10 am–5 pm; admission $6.50

Kananaskis Country (104/B5)
An idyllic holiday resort around 100 km (62 miles) west of Calgary on the sunny, heavily wooded East side of the Rocky Mountains. The Olympic down hill races were held on Mount Allan in 1988. There are an excellent golf course and a wide network of bicycle and hiking trails.

Spruce Meadows (104/B5)
One of the world's largest equestrian centres, ranking second only after Aachen/Germany. A must for fans of show jumping. *RR#9, Calgary, T2J 5G5; Tel: (403) 974-4200*

EDMONTON

(104/C4) Fur traders, gold rush, oil boom — the provincial capital of Alberta has seen it all, and it has developed into a metropolis of more than 880,000 inhabitants today. The oil industry is the principal source of employment alongside the government offices. In the east and south of the city in particular thousands of pumps pump Alberta's "black gold" into the pipelines. There is littleindustry in the city itself however, the dead straight roads, in the typicl grid formation, are lined with well-tended residential areas, shining high rise offices dominate the city centre. There are lots of lakes round about to attract fishermen and visitors can ride to their heart's content on the old ranches. So, despite the icy cold winters, the city provides a good quality of life for its inhabitants. From the tourist's point of view, Edmonton, with its international airport, is principally a base for tours of the Rockies and — via the Alaska Highway — into the far North of Canada.

SIGHTSEEING

In the modern city centre, on a hill above the charming valley of the North Saskatchewan River with its green areas, life centres around *Sir Winston Churchill Square* with its art galleries and theatres. The main shopping street is *Jasper Avenue.* Down on the river bank, it's worth visiting *Muttart Conservatory,* a botanical garden, with four futuristic glass pyramids which impressively offset the city centre skyline.

The traditional North-American skyline — here in Edmonton

MUSEUMS

Fort Edmonton Park
The extensive open air museum on the river bank displays the history of the city fromfur trading days to the 20th century. The Hudson's Bay Company fort of 1845 was been reconstructed in accurate detail.

Whitemud Freeway, in summer daily 10 am–6 pm; admission: $6.75

Provincial Museum
Indian culture, pioneer history and the particularly impressive world of the dinosaur.

12845 102nd Av., in summer daily 9 am–5 pm; other times Tues–Sun 9 am–5 pm; admission: $6.50

Space & Science Centre
In fact it is Canada's biggest planetarium with a laser show and space films in the exciting Imax cinema.

111th Av./142nd St., in summer daily 10 am–10 pm; admission: $7; Imax cinema $7

RESTAURANTS

Bistro Praha
◈ Pretty, small bistro with Czech food in the heart of the city.

10168 100 A St.; Tel: (403) 424-4218; Category 3

Bones
Popular steak restaurant in the city centre. Very good ribs.

10220 103rd St.; Tel: (403) 421-4747; Category 2

Hardware Grill
Indisputably the best restaurant in the city. Modern Canadian food with lots of regional specialities. Chic atmosphere in historical setting and good wines.

9698 Jasper Av.; Tel: (403) 423-0969; Category 1-2

SHOPPING

West Edmonton Mall
★ The biggest shopping centre in the world — both shoppers' paradise and visitor attraction. More

than 800 shops and restaurants, a big amusement park, an artificial lake (with submarines!) and even a wave pool — all under one roof. Not to be missed!
87th Av./170th St.

HOTELS

Fantasyland
An unique collection of kitsch: Each of the 355 rooms has a different theme — Arabia, Hollywood or the South Seas.
17700 87th Av.; Tel: (403) 444-3000; Fax: 444-3294; Category 1

Glenora B & B Inn
Good B & B near to the city centre, antique furnishings.
11 rooms, 12327 102nd Av.; Tel: (403) 488-6766; Fax: 488-5168; Category 2–3

Macdonald
Splendidly renovated grand hotel dating back to 1915. Lots of rooms with beautiful ☆☆ views over the river.
198 rooms, 10065 100th St.; Tel: (403) 424-5181; Fax: 424-8017; Category 1

Royal Inn
Reliable middle category hotel near West Edmonton Mall. Good bistro.
194 rooms, 10010 178th St.; Tel: (403) 484-6000; Fax: 489-2900; Category 2–3

ENTERTAINMENT

As well as the usual bars and nightclubs in the big hotels in the city centre, nighthawks should head for Old Strathcona in the university district on the south bank of the Saskatchewan River. Around

82nd Avenue (called Whyte Avenue here) are numerous cafes, restaurants and music bars. Western music fans should head for ★ ☆ *Cook County Saloon (8010 103rd St.).* Jazz fans will find good bands at *Yardbird Suite (10203 106th Av.).*

INFORMATION

Edmonton Tourism
9797 Jasper Av. NW, Edmonton, AB T5J 2Z4; Tel: (403) 496-8400; Fax: 425-5283

SURROUNDING AREA

Elk Island National Park (104/C4)
This 200 sq km (77 sq mi) park about 40 km (25 mi) east of Edmonton provides a protected environment for a large herd of Prairie bison, moose, elks and more than 200 species of birds.

Reynolds-Alberta Museum (104/C4)
The big museum complex just 60 km (38 miles) south of Edmonton is mainly dedicated to the first half of the 20th century in Western Canada: agricultural equipment and old aeroplanes, vintage cars and historic films.
Wetaskiwin, on Hwy. 13, in summer 9 am 7pm, other times to 5 pm; admission $6.50

FORT MACLEOD

(104/C6) The nostalgic farming-town (3000 pop.) on the Oldman River is one of the oldest settlements in the West. In 1874 a section of the Northwest Mounted Police arrived here to set up a fort, to try to stop the whisky-trade with the Indians — the first outpost of white civilisation in the then still very wild West.

Fort Macleod Museum

In the (reconstructed) police fort students in the historic bright red uniforms of the Canadian police put on riding displays every day during the summer.

25th St./3rd Av.; in summer daily 9 am–8.30 pm; other times: 9.30 am– 4 pm; admission $4

Head-Smashed-In Buffalo Jump

★ The name says it all: this is where the Indians drove the bison herds over a steep cliff. The women waited at the bottom to cut the animals up and dry the meat for winter supplies. The excellent museum just 20 km west of Fort Macleod in the Blackfoot Indian reservation tells of the life and hunting methods of the Prairie Indians.

Hwy. 785, in summer daily 9 am-8 pm; other times to 5pm; admission $6.50

FORT MCMURRAY

(105/D2) Some 35,000 workers prospect for oil in the wilderness of North Alberta. Scientists calculate that there are 500 billion barrels under the ground here. Since the sixties a modern mining town has grown up as a result, in

The bison in Elk Island National Park are looked after and well cared for

the middle of the endless forests on the Athabasca River. If you're interested in technology, make the long journey from Edmonton to the ultra-modern *Oil Sands Interpretive Centre* to learn about the extraction of oil from the sedimentary rock. *Victoria Day to Labour Day daily 10 m–6 pm; other times 12 noon to 5 pm; admission $3*

MEDICINE HAT

(**105/D6**) The biggest city in the southeast of Alberta (43,000 pop.) owes its existence mainly to the natural gas industry and is both an important stopping point on the Trans-Canada Highway and a supply centre for the farms in the wide area round about. The strange name of the city is supposed to stem from the era of the wars with the Blackfoot and Cree Indians, when a Cree medicine man lost his head-dress in battle, resulting in a bloody defeat for his tribe.

SURROUNDING AREA

Cypress Hills Provincial Park (**105/D6**)
The Cypress Hills tower up over the prairies, southeast of Medicine Hat — a green oasis in the distant plain. During the Ice Ages the region was not covered by glaciers and so the vegetation which survived there is very untypical of the prairies. Trailsand campsites invite the visitor to spend time here. At theLoch Leven tourist centre you can rent bicycles and canoes.

Dinosaur Provincial Park (**105/D5**)
The bed of the Red Deer River northwest of Medicine Hat is

one of the best places in the world for finding dinosaur fossils. 35 species of primeval saurian have already been found here. Unesco has declared the region a world heritage centre. Educational trails and bus tours are available to the excavation sites. The Visitor Centre displays a selection of findings.

LETHBRIDGE

(**104/C6**) With a good 60,000 inhabitants, this farming settlement is the most important city in south Alberta. In *Indian Battle Park* on the western edge of the city is *Fort Whoop-up,* with its reputation dating back to the Pioneer era, where American whisky traders deceived the Indians to get their furs. *(June-Aug daily 10 am–6 pm, Sun 12–5 pm).*

Nearby the *Coal Banks Interpretive Center* illustrates the history of coal mining in the region. Rather out of place here in the prairie but nevertheless worth a visit, *Nikko Yuko Japanese Gardens,* are well-kept traditional Japanese style gardens *(Middle May to middle October daily 9 am 8 pm).*

SURROUNDING AREA

Writing on Stone Provincial Park (**104/C6**)
Hoodoos, stone pillars strangely deformed by the wind and weather, are the attraction in the Milk River valley south of Lethbridge. The region was sacred to the Indians and they left behind lots of rock drawings.
In summer daily guided tours; Tel: (403) 647-2364

On the trail of Jack London

The Arctic, one of the last wilderness regions on earth

For wilderness fans and friends of nature alike the region north of the 60th parallel is the most beautiful part of Canada. It is harsh, largely undeveloped country, where austere beauty and misanthropic nature provide a great deal of material for stories of trappers and Gold Diggers and failed expeditions. And it is also a huge region. The Northern Territories, with an area of 3.9 mill. sq km (1.5 mill. sq mi), cover a good third of the area of the whole of Canada.

Politically the North is divided into two territories: the mountainous Yukon Territory in the West, which just 100 years ago experienced the biggest Gold Rush of all time in the Klondike, and the much bigger Northwest Territories, which stretch from Hudson Bay to the North Pole. Only about 30,000 people live in the Yukon Territory, and about 60,000 in the Northwest Territories. The majority of them are Dene Indians and Inuit, who have recently held talks with the Federal Government concerning the return of their

Can-can girls in Dawson City are as easy-going these days as the atmosphere

land. It is already agreed that on 1 April 1999 the northeastern part of the Northwest Territories will come under the independent control of the Inuit people.

Good equipment and accurate planning are vital to survival in a tour of the North, even though it is pleasantly warm here in summer (up to 30 °C/86 °F). The easiest option is to travel in the area around Great Slave Lake (**108/B–C5**) and in Yukon Territory (**106–107/B1–E6**), where there are roads and a tourist infrastructure. Here you will find glacier covered mountainranges and the huge valleys of the Yukon and Mackenzie Rivers.

The most important North country route is made up of the Alaska Highway, built during the Second World War, (now completely asphalted) and the Mackenzie Highway from Edmonton to Yellowknife along Great Slave Lake. Metalled wilderness trails lead from these into the surrounding country – the Liard Highway to Nahanni National Park, the Klondike Highway to Jack London's historic Gold Rush country around Dawson City.

The other Arctic regions can only be reached by plane. The

MARCO POLO SELECTION: THE NORTHERN TERRITORIES

1 Dempster Highway
700 kilometres (440 miles)
wilderness route from
Dawson City to the Mack-
enzie delta (page 85)

**2 Prince of Wales
Northern Heritage Centre**
Pioneer history
and native culture
(page 88)

small Inuit settlements are linked to the outside world by scheduled flights once or twice a week, the remote wilderness lodges for animal watching are only accessible by bush plane.

ATLIN, B.C.

(102/B1) It is mainly because of its wonderful mountain-ringed location on the lake of the same name, that Atlin is worth the roughly 100 km (62 mile) diversion from the Alaska Highway. The picturesquely dilapidated gold diggers' settlement, founded in 1898 during the big Klondike Gold Rush, is actually in British Columbia but is only accessible from the Yukon Territory. About 500 people live in and around Atlin: Gold diggers, artists, dropouts. One thing you must do here: a flight over the glacier covered Coast Mountains, for example with *Summit Air Charter, Tel: (250) 651-76 00.*

DAWSON CITY

(106/A4) The Gold Rush era still lives on in this almost ghost town, once known as the "Paris of the North". About 30,000 people lived here at the time of

Atlin Lake serves as a base for flights

the Klondike Gold Rush in 1900: adventurers and dancing girls, engineers and saloon owners. Boardwalk pavements and dilapidated wooden frontages still give Dawson the Wild West look. In *Diamond Tooth Gertie's Gambling Hall* the can-can girls still dance, in the *Palace Grand Theatre* melodramas are performed, and in *Jack London's cabin* a resurrected Jack reads from his novels. You can look round lots of the renovated old buildings, like the *Post Office* on King Street, *Harrington's Store* on 3rd Avenue (photo exhibition) or the historic *paddle steamer "S.S. Keno"* on the shore of the Yukon River. The best view of the city is from the ❧ *Midnight Dome,* reached by climbing a gravel road to the top of the hill.

The town (1700 pop.) at the mouth of the Klondike River in the Yukon now survives through tourism but in the area around, even today, some die-hards still prospect for gold. And there are still wild celebrations in the saloons on Saturday nights when the miners come into town to celebrate the week's successes.

MUSEUM

Dawson City Museum
Historical photos and all kinds of mining equipment illustrate the town's golden era. Films and gold panning every day.
5th Av./Church St., in summer daily 10 am–6pm; admission $3.25

RESTAURANT

Klondike Kate's
Pleasant restaurant in a historical building with nice terrace. Exten-

sive menu and very good coffee.
3rd Av./King St.; Tel: (867) 993-6527; Category 2

HOTELS

Dawson City Bunkhouse
Simple rooms in a new but old-style building. No en-suite.
16 rooms; Princess St.; Bag 4040; Tel: (867) 993-6164; Fax: 993-6051, Category 2

Eldorado
The first house in Dawson – whatever that means. The 52 rooms are modern and comfortable, but not overly luxurious, Restaurant and saloon.
3rd Av./Princess St.; Tel: (867) 993-5451; Fax: 993-5256; Category 1

INFORMATION

Visitor Reception Centre
The visitor centre offers a slide show and guided tours of the town.
Front St./King St.; Tel: (867) 993-5462; Fax: 993-5683

SURROUNDING AREA

Bonanza Creek   (106/B4)
The first gold was discovered in this side valley of the Klondike River in August 1896. Huge slag heaps and an enormous old gold panning system, Dredge No. 4, are testimony to the hard work of the Gold Diggers.

Dempster Highway   (106/B4–C2)
★ This wilderness road runs over 700 km (440 miles) from Dawson City through largely unpopulated Tundra north across the Polar Circle to the Inuit settlement of Inuvik in the Mackenzie

delta. Two small Indian villages and one petrol station are all you pass on the road side all the way along, otherwise nothing but Arctic wilderness. The journey is particularly beautiful at the beginning of September when the leaves are changing colour.

HAINES JUNCTION

(106/B6) The tiny village in the middle of the mountains on the Alaska Highway is a base for tours in the *Kluane National Park,* a good 22,000 sq km (8,500 sq mi) largely undeveloped mountain wilderness. Here, in the ice-covered St. Elias Mountains is *Mt. Logan,* at 5,959 m (19,665 ft) the highest mountain in Canada. At the Visitor Centre in the National Park here you can see an excellent slide show, the rangers can provide tips for hiking and rafting tours on the glacier rivers.

TOURS

Kluane Park Adventure Center
Central booking office for riding, walking and rafting tours in the wilderness of the Park.
P.O. Box 5479, Haines Junction, YT Y0B 1L0; Tel und Fax: (867) 634-2313

HOTELS

Cozy Corner Motel
Simple, reliable motel on the Highway. Restaurant in the motel.
12 rooms; P.O. Box 5406, Haines Junction, Tel: (867) 634-2511; Fax: 634-2119; Category 2

Dalton Trail Lodge
Very well-kept lodge run by Swiss owners, about 40 km (25 miles)

In the casino in Dawson City

south of the village at the edge of the Kluane National Park. Canoe trips and horse-back riding.
15 rooms; P.O. Box 5331, Haines Junction; Tel/Fax: (867) 667-1099; Category 2

INUVIK

(106/C2) A small town that looks as if it is made out of building bricks. The houses of the biggest town in the western Arctic are as brighly coloured as Easter eggs. Around 3,000 people – Inuit, Dene and white – live here on the eastern edge of the huge Mackenzie delta and do credit to the name of the town which means "place of man". If you are bold enough to make the journey 700 km (440 miles) from Dawson City on Dempster Highway, it is worth taking a *plane trip* into the surrounding area. Perhaps to the trapper town of *Aklavik* in the middle of the 80 km (50 mile) wide river delta, or to the old *whale catching station on Herschel Island,* or to the *Inuit settlement of Tuktoyaktuk* on the Arctic Ocean coast. In the town itself, the igloo shaped *church* is worth seeing.

TOURS

Arctic Nature Tours

Plane excursions to the Macken-zie delta, Herschel Island and to the National Parks in the nort-hern Yukon Territory.
P. O. Box 1530, Inuvik; Tel: (867) 979-3300, Fax: 979-3400

NAHANNI NATIONAL PARK

(**107/D–E5**) A Park for white-water freaks. The South Nahanni River flows through the Mackenzie Mo-untains for 320 km (200 miles), rushes over the 90 m (294 ft) high *Virginia Falls* and foams through up to 900 m (2,900 ft) deep canyons. Guided canoe tour and wilderness expeditions from Whitehorse, for example with *Nahanni River Ad-ventures, P.O. Box 4869, Whitehorse, YT Y1A 4N6; Tel: (867) 668-3180; Fax: 668-3056.*

WATSON LAKE

(**107/D6**) Since the construction of the Alaska Highway in 1942 the town (1700 pop.) in the southern Yukon Territory has been an im-portant supply post, The *Watson Lake Signpost Forest,* a forest of signposts from all over the world, started 50 years ago by a homesick soldier, also dates back to this time. Immediately next to it, a modern *Interpretive Centre* shows the history of the Alaska Highway.

WHITEHORSE

(**106/B6**) On the wide bank of the Yukon River stretches the busy capital (23,00 pop.) of the Yukon Territory. In the *MacBride*

Museum and the *Old Log Church Museum* you can experience the golden age of the town around 1900, when thousands of gold diggers came through Miles Canyon on rafts and home-made boats to get to the Klondike gold fields. The *"S.S. Klondike",* a nostalgic and lovingly restored paddle steamer of the Gold Era is also on show. Along the narrow gauge tracksof the *White Pass & Yukon Railway* during the sum-mer, an excursion train steams from Whitehorse (bus connec-tion) through the Coast Moun-tains to the old Gold Rush port of *Skagway* in Alaska.

SHOPPING

Murdoch's

Jewellery made from gold nug-gets. *207 Main St.*

Northern Images

Good quality Inuit sculptures, prints and fur parkas, made by the Inuit in their small villages on the Arctic Ocean Coast.
311 Jarvis St.

TOURS

Canoe People

Equipment for canoe trips on the Yukon to Dawson City, also gui-ded tours.
P. O. Box 5152, Whitehorse YT Y1A 4S3; Tel: (867) 668-4899; Fax: 668-4891

HOTELS

Edgewater

Small, modern hotel in the centre.
30 rooms; 101 Main Street; Tel: (867) 667-2572; Fax: 668-3014; Category 2

Town & Mountain

Modern hotel in the centre with restaurant and bar.

30 rooms: 401 Main Street; Tel: (867) 668-7644; Fax: 668-5822; Category 2

INFORMATION

Tourism Yukon

P.O. Box 2703, Whitehorse, YT Y1A 2C6; Tel: (867) 667-5340; Fax: 667-3546

WOOD BUFFALO NATIONAL PARK

(108/B–C6) With 45,000 sq km (17,000 sq mi) this protected area in the Peace River and Athabasca River delta is bigger than Switzerland. The endless forests are the home of a free-roaming *bison herd* of over 3,000 animals. Numerous *water birds* nest in the marshy areas, including rare whooping cranes and pelicans. Visitor centre at Fort Smith. From Fort Smith there are some metalled tracks into the protected area and you can take a *boat trip* on the Slave River.

YELLOWKNIFE

(108/B4) The *Pilot's Monument,* on a bare rocky dome, offers the best ◁▷ view over the modern capital of the Northwest Territories on the shore of the Great Slave Lake. The 15,000 inhabitants are employed in administative offices or in the two gold mines, which extract the coveted metal from the ancient rock of the Canadian Shield. But gold alone is not responsible for the present boom in Yellowknife. Diamonds have

recently been discovered north of the town.

MUSEUM

Prince of Wales Northern Heritage Centre

★ In unquestionably the best museum in the Northwest Territories you can see exhibitions of Arctic flora and fauna and excellent Inuit sculptures.

Frame Lake St./48th St., 10.30 am– 5 pm daily; in winter: closed Mondays; admission free

RESTAURANT

The Wildcat Cafe

Hearty pioneer food and caribou steaks in the Old Town.

Tel: (867) 873-8850, Category 2

HOTELS

Bathurst Inlet Lodge   (E1)

Wilderness lodge on the coast of the Arctic Ocean 600 km (375 mi) away, excellent for animal watching. Book a few months in advance. Own plane service from and to Yellowknife.

10 rooms; P.O. Box 820, Yellow-knife, NWT X1A 2N6; Tel: (867) 873-2595; Fax: 920-4263; Category 1

Discovery Inn

Modern hotel in the city centre.

41 rooms, 4701 Franklin Av.; Tel: (867) 873-4151; Fax: 920-7948; Category 2

INFORMATION

NWT Arctic Tourism

Box 9600, Yellowknife, NWT X1A 2L9; Tel: (867) 873-7200; Fax: 873-0294

On the trail of the trappers

These routes are marked in green on the map inside front flap and in the road atlas beginning on page 100

① PRAIRIES, MOUNTAINS AND THE OCEAN: FROM EAST TO WEST

An introductory tour, ideal for first time visitors. In 8–10 days you can experience the diversity of the landscape of Western Canada: from the prairies around Calgary to the ice-covered peaks of the Rocky Mountains, from the forest-covered lake areas in the heart of British Columbia to the Pacific Coast in Vancouver. And there's time for hiking, canoe excursions or horse-back riding at one of the ranches on the way. You could also join this route up with one of the following routes to make a longer circular trip. The best time of year for the 1500 km (940 miles) journey: June to the beginning of October.

Calgary (page 71) is worth a whole day — to see the museums and for a shopping trip in the modern malls in the city centre. Then it's off again, heading west into the wide expanse of the country. The *Trans-Canada Highway* runs along Bow River through the old tribal territory of the Blackfoot Indians from the prairies into the mountains. If you've got children with you, it's worth stopping off in the softly undulating ranchcountry at *Seebe* at the

Rafter Six Ranch (Indian museum, horse-back riding).

At *Canmore* the mountains creep nearer to Hwy. 1, and you soon see — immediately after the first sign warning of bears — the entrance to *Banff National Park (page 62)*, the oldest and most famous protected area in the Rockies. You should allow two nights at *Banff (page 63)* or in *Lake Louise (page 63)* to allow time for walks in the mountains — at *Moraine Lake (page 65)* or in *Johnston Canyon*. And when you're at Lake Louise, make sure you visit the less well-known *Yoho National Park (page 71)*, where the highest waterfalls in the Rockies spray out of the Wapta ice field.

On further north: for the drive along ◆ *Icefields Parkway (page 63)* you'll need to take some extra rolls of film. Of particular beauty are the narrow gorge of the *Mistaya River* and the wonderful panoramic view on *Water-fowl Lake (trails)*. After a steep climb to 2035 m (6715 ft) high *Sunwapta Pass* an approximately two hour walk is recommended in good weather on the *Parker Ridge Trail*, before the route crosses the *Athabasca* glacier *(page 66)* into *Jasper National Park (page 66)*. It's worth stopping here for a day too — to walk in *Maligne Canyon* and take a boat trip on *Maligne Lake (page 66)*.

Highway 16 runs westwards over the border to British Columbia (time difference: minus 1h). With luck it will be sunny and *Mount Robson (page 68)*, the highest peak in the Canadian Rocky Mountains, will be showing off its majestic ice-covered summit.

Now it gets quite isolated. From *Valemount,* a heli-skiing centre in winter, Hwy. 5 passes south through completely uninhabited mountain regions in the west of the Rockies. Only every 50 or 80 km (30 or 50 mi) will you pass a settlement or a petrol station. After a visit to the waterfalls in the equally remote *Wells Gray Provincial Park (page 57)* you reach civilisation once again in the ranch country around *Kamloops (page 52)*.

In the Thompson River valley the *Trans-Canada Highway* snakes further west. Here, in the 'interior' of B.C., in countryside like you see in Westerns, it is almost as dry as the desert. You could visit *Hat Creek Ranch* at *Cache Creek:* a preserved mail coach station. There's even more pioneer spirit in *Lillooet (page 50)*, a traditional pioneer town at the beginning of *Caribou Road,* the old 19th century gold diggers' route. The wooden frontages on the main street and the gallow tree on the slope above the town recall the wild days of yesteryear.

From Lillooet the route follows the Fraser River to the sea.

The river has carved a deep canyon through the Coast Mountains. The narrowest and wildest section is south of *Lytton (page 53)*. Next stop: *Hope,* a pioneer town which achieved cinematic fame in the eighties when Sylvester Stallone filmed the action classic 'Rambo' here. By the time you get to Hope it is already greener and damper. Dense forests cover the mountainslopes and follow Hwy. 1 through the ever widening Fraser Valley to the end of the journey in *Vancouver (page 31)*.

② THE SOUTH: FORESTS AND QUIET LAKES

A route for the connoisseur: the sunny south of the provinces is ideal for a pleasant holiday spent by long lakes and in Wild West villages. And there's no shortage of attractions for nature lovers. Along the route are National Parks such as Waterton Lakes, historic sites like Fort Steele and ghost towns from the gold rush era. Time needed for the 1,900 km (1,200 mi) long route: 10 days.

From *Vancouver (page 31)* the route first runs east through the wide, fertile Fraser Valley. To prepare you for a journey into pioneer country: a stop at the historic site of *Fort Langley (page 37)*, where you're taken back to the time of the fur traders. Flower fans should visit the *Minter Gardens* in *Chilliwack*.

From the town of *Hope* Hwy. 3 climbs up into the Coast Mountains to the forest covered *Manning Provincial Park,* where wild rhododendron bushes flower magnificently in spring *(hiking and riding trails)*. From the 1346 m (4440 ft) high *Allison*

Pass you drop down to the dry, sunny east side of the mountains in the Similka Valley. Fruit orchards line the floor of the valley and farmers sell cherries and peaches. Worth a visit: the small *museum* in the Grist Mill in *Keremeos,* which shows the life of the pioneers.

Osoyoos (page 55) is near the US border and, with all the bathers on the shores of *Osoyoos Lake* it looks like a Mediterranean holiday resort. The route now follows the *Okanagan Valley (page 54)* north – past sandy bathing beaches, orchards and vineyards.

North of *Vernon* it soon becomes quieter and more peaceful as you travel along the Trans-Canada Highway. Deep in the forests of the Monashee Mountains is a historic stopping point: *Craigellachie,* the railway station where the last nail was hammered into the Trans-Canadian Railway on 9 November 1885.

When you're in *Mt. Revelstoke National Park (page 54)* make sure you take a trip up to the flowermeadows on the peak. Then back to Hwys. 23, 31 and 3A to travel south into the *Arrow Lakes (page 54)* region – scarcely developed pioneer country with small, remote villages, marvellous Provincial Parks in isolated mountain scenery and long lakes, which the Highways cross by means of car ferries. Worthwhile stops on the way: the *hot springs* at *Nakusp (page 54)* and *Ainsworth,* the small ghosttown of *Sandon (page 54)* from the silver boom era around 1890 and the picturesque old mining town of *Nelson (page 28).* In the *Kokanee*

Creek Provincial Park you can watch the salmon spawning in August.

Back across the US border, the route continues (time difference: + 1h) to *Cranbrook* (big railway museum) and to the historical site of *Fort Steele* near *Kimberley (page 68).* In the East you can now see the dramatic peaks of the Rocky Mountains rearing up and Hwy. 3 crosses them at 1396 m (4607 ft) at *Crowsnest Pass (page 66).*

The *Frank Slide Visitor Center* shows you the harsh life of the coal miners at the end of the 19th century.

At *Pincher Creek* the Highway heads out into the endless prairie – but first another trip south: into the magnificent mountain scenery of the *Waterton Lakes National Park (page 70),* with its boat trips and trails. Then out of the mountains and through *Fort Macleod page 79)* with its excellent *Indian Museum* and north through the ranch country of Alberta to the end of the tour – the oil metropolis of *Calgary (page 74).*

③ THE WEST COAST: FJORDS AND GREEN ISLANDS

The jagged Pacific coast along the famous Inside Passage and the almost completely undeveloped North of British Columbia are the highlights of this route. A journey into the homelands of the Indians, lumberjacks and pioneer farmers – where the West is still wild and untamed. Distance: 2,400 km (1,500 miles) not including ferry crossings. Time required: approx. 2 weeks. Important note: book the ferry crossing from Port Hardy to Prince Rupert.

From the ferry port of *Tsaw-wassen* on the southern fringes of *Vancouver (page 31)* car ferries leave for *Vancouver Island (page 39)* every hour. First stop on the island: the bright and colourful *Butchart Gardens (page 47)*. It's not far from here to *Victoria (page 44)*, with its excellent Provincial Museum and pretty old town, which make it well worth spending a day here.

As you continue along the Trans-Canada Highway, you pass right next to *Goldstream Park,* where the salmon swim to their spawning ground in late summer and die in the shallow water — in an impressive natural drama. It's a day's journey — past bathing beaches and holiday resorts like *Chemainus (page 42)* — to the West Coast of Vancouver Island: to the *Pacific Rim National Park (page 43)*. The fishing town of *Tofino* is the best place to spend a day walking on the beach and perhaps taking a boat or kayak trip.

Back on the East Coast, the route then follows Hwy. 19 across *Campbell River (page 40)* to the north of Vancouver Island. Not to be missed: a trip to watch the whales from *Telegraph Cove (page 44)* and a trip to *Alert Bay (page 40)*, where you can admire the wonderful collection of totem poles and Indian masks.

Next morning: board the boat at *Port Hardy (page 44)* for the journey through the *Inside Passage (page 44)*, the old Gold Diggers' route through the maze of islands off the West Coast — hopefully in sunshine. It usually rains here, as the steep Coast Mountains trap the Pacific clouds. But this also has its ad-

vantages: a unique *ancient forest* of towering Douglas firs and sitka spruces flourishes here. Whether it's sunny or raining, keep your eyes open — because you can often see whales, seals and bald eagles from the ferry.

Prince Rupert (page 59), the ferry port at the north end of the Inside Passage, lies in the territory of the Tsimshian Indians. All over the town huge totem poles testify to their carving skills *(exhibitions in the Visitors Bureau)*. And of course the fish in the port is excellent to eat, especially the halibut. The *North Pacific Cannery Museum* in the suburb of *Port Edward* documents the local fishing tradition.

The next part of the journey on the *Yellowhead Highway (page 58)* leads along the often cloud covered Skeena River to *Hazelton (page 59)*, a large Tsimshian settlement. Here you can take a short trip to Alaska. It's about a half day's journey on the Cassiar Highway to *Stewart (page 59)*, right on the border.

Isolated forests and lakes, only the odd pioneer farm or village — it's a lonely journey along Yellowhead Highway. Not until *Prince George (page 59)* do large deforested areas once again reveal man's impact on nature.

On Hwy. 16 after Prince George you can join up with the first route and carry on to the Rockies. To go back south, take Hwy. 97 through the *Caribou region (page 50)*. Don't miss the old gold rush town of *Barkerville (page 50)*, now a museum. In *Cache Creek* our route takes us by retourning on the first route to the Trans Canada Highway right on the way back to Vancouver.

Practical information

Useful addresses and indispensable tips for your visit to Western Canada

BANK, MONEY AND CREDIT CARDS

The national currency is the Canadian Dollar (= 100 Cents). There are 5, 10, 20, 50 und 100 Dollar bank notes and 1c (penny), 5c (nickel), 10c (dime), 25c (quarter), $1 and $2 coins.

Banks are usually open from 10 am to 3 pm. They change *travellers' cheques* (made out in Canadian $) but do not change foreign currencies. Only the airports and lots of the bigger hotels will change foreign currencies into dollars (at unfavourable rates). You should take your *holiday money* in several forms: approx. 100 dollars *cash* for when you arrive, *travellers' cheques* in Can$ (these are accepted everywhere in shops and restaurants, and you get your change in cash) for day to day expenses and a *credit card* (Visa or Eurocard) for bigger purchases and emergencies. *Eurocheques are not accepted.*

CAMPING

The public campsites are the most beautiful: close to nature, on lakesides and in National Parks, and equipped with campfire facilities, wooden benches, water pumps and latrine. The cost is $5-14 per night. Private, often luxuriously equipped sites with hot showers, swimming pools and shops can be found on the outskirts of towns and outside the Parks (rates: approx. $10-30). Camping in the wild is not forbidden — except in the Parks — but it is not looked on favourably in populated areas.

CAR RENTAL

Minimum age is 21 or 25. A national driving licence is sufficient. You should book cars or campers several months in advance at your travel bureau. This is much cheaper and safer than trying do do it once you're there as mobile homes in particular are very popular in the high season. It is advisable to return your vehicle to your starting point as the vehicle return charge is often very high.

CLIMATE

Apart from the coastal region of British Columbia the climate in Western Canada is an extreme Continental climate, with guaranteed snow in the cold winters and often surprisingly hot summers. The best season for travelling (also the high seaon) is the middle of June to the end of August. But September is often just as lovely – with clear sunny days and cold nights. At the end of the month, in the Indian summer the leaves of the birches and poplars start to turn. Skiing in the Rockies is best in February and March.

CONSULATES

British Consulate
800-1111 Melville, Vancouver, British Columbia V6E 2M6; Tel: (604) 683-4421

United States Consulate
1059 West Pender Street, Vancouver, British Columbia V6E 2M6; Tel: (604) 685-4311

CUSTOMS

You cannot take plants, sausages and other fresh foods into Canada. The allowance for each adult is 200 cigarettes or 50 cigars or 14 oz tobacco, as well as 1.1l spirits. Also gifts up to a value of 60 Can$ per person. The duty-free allowance to the UK is: 200 cigarettes or 50 cigars, 1 l alcohol over 22%, 2l wine, 60ml perfume, 250ml eau de toilette, other goods to a value of 136£. The following can be taken into the US duty free: 1l alcohol, 200 cigarettes, 100 cigars, goods to the value of 100$.

DRIVING

You national driver's licence is adequate for trips up to three months (one month in Yukon Territory). In all provinces it is compulsory to *wear a seat belt. Maximum speed* usually 80 or 100 kmh (50 or 62 mph) on major roads, 50 kmh (30 mph) in towns, 110 kmh (69 mph) on motorways. Traffic regulations are the same as in Europe. But there are a few *differences:* At the traffic lights you can turn right even when the lights are red. Overtaking on the right is permitted on multi-lane roads. You are not allowed to pass school buses with their warning lights on – even if you're going in the opposite direction. In the Yukon Territory you have to drive with your headlights on all the time.

The *Canadian Automobile Association (CAA)* is always prepared to help members of other automobile associations (take your membership card along).

HEALTH

British citizens are recommended to take out a one year travel insurance policy, which covers common illnesses. American citizens should ensure that their health insurance policy covers them outside the US.

HUNTING AND FISHING

There is a local guide to hunting in all the provinces: information available from travel offices. But fishing in the many lakes and rivers is very simple: depending on the province, a licence, which is obtainable from all sports shopsand lodges, costs the visitor $ 10–30. In the National Parks fishing is only permitted with a special licence.

INFORMATION

In the UK:

Canada Tourism Program general information can be obtained from the following address:

Visit Canada Center
62–65 Trafalgar Square, London WC2 5DY; Tel: 08917/715-000

In Canada:

Travellers from the US or Canada should contact the following regional travel offices:

Tourism British Columbia
802–865 Hornby Street; Vancouver, British Columbia, Canada V6Z 2G3; Tel: (604) 660-2861 or (800) 663-6000

Tourism Yukon
Box 2703; Whitehorse; Yukon, Canada Y1A 2C6; Tel: (867) 667 5340

Northwest Territories Tourism
Box 1320; Yellowknife; Northwest Territories, Canada 1A 2L9; Tel: (800) 661-0788

Travel Alberta
Box 2500; Edmonton; Alberta, Canada T5J 2Z4; Tel: (800) 661-8888
In Canada you will find well posted — information centres and visitor centres in every National Park and even the smallest village, where you can obtain maps and more detailed information.

INTERNAL FLIGHTS AND FERRIES

Canadian Airlines, Air Canada and many regional airlines offer up to 40% reduction on the inland flights. But you have to book these flights along with your return tickets. The major European airlines will do it for you, too.

The generally hourly ferry service between Vancouver Island and the mainland does not have to be booked in advance. But it is highly recommended that you book as early as possible for the 15 hour ferry crossing through the famous Inside Passage between Port Hardy and Prince Rupert (available from *B.C. Ferries, 1112 Fort Street, Victoria, British Columbia, Canada V8V 4V2, Tel: (250) 386-3431 or (604) 669-1211*).

OPENING HOURS

Shops are generally open Monday to Saturday from 9.30 am until 6 pm. The big shopping malls in the cities from 10 am until 9 pm and Sundays from 12 noon until 5 pm. Supermarkets are generally also open in the evenings and at weekends, and in the big cities they can be open 24 hours a day. Most museums are closed on Mondays.

PASSPORTS

Permanent residents of the United States do not need a passport or any other immigration documents but need to have proof of identity (green card or naturalisation certificate). American citizens entering Canada from countries other than the US need a valid passport, naturalisation certificate or green card.

British citizens only need a valid passport for a maximum stay of six months.

POST & TELEPHONE

Post offices are open Monday through Friday from 9 am until 6 pm and on Saturdays from 8 am until 12 noon. Postage for air mail letters or postcards to Europe is 90c. It takes around five days for a postcard to reach its destination from the big cities and around nine days from rural areas.

All *telephone numbers* in Canada are seven digit numbers, with a three digit code in front for long distance calls *(area code)*. For British Columbia the area code is 250, for Vancouver 604, for Alberta 403, for Yukon and Northwest Territories 867.

Local calls from a telephone box cost 25c. In the case of *long distance calls* a computer voice tells you the applicable rate after you have dialled. Hotels often charge horrendous rates for calls. If you have any telephone problems, the *operator* (dial '0') will be glad to help. The operator also connects *reverse charge calls.* There are also *freecall numbers* with the prefix 800 or 888, which you can use to book hotels or car rental.

When calling from Canada and the US, the code for the United Kingdom is 011 44.

The code for Canada from the UK is 001.

TAXES

A tax of 7%, known as GST, applies throughout Canada. Hotel taxes and in British Columbia a regional tax of 7% are applied in addition to this. All taxes are added at the time of payment.

TIME ZONES

The time difference in British Columbia and Yukon Territory compared with Western Europe is minus eight hours, in Alberta minus seven hours (time zone boundary is usually the spine of the Rocky Mountains). Summer time (plus one hour) applies from first Sunday in April to last Sunday in October.

TIPPING

Service charge is not included in restaurant bills. You should therefore leave around 15% of the bill total on the table. You should give the hotel porter about $1–2 per item of luggage.

TRAVEL

Greyhound and several regional bus companies (like Brewster, Pacific Western Transportation, Red Arrow) run regular services between all the major towns. Information (including info on the Ameripass card) is available from travel bureaus.

If you're taking the *train,* a journey through Canada can be a particularly wonderful experience on the legendary Trans-Canada route from Montreal to Vancouver or on the excursion train, the *Rocky Mountaineer,* from Calgary to Vancouver (it is recommended that you book several months in advance). The railway company VIA-Rail offers a Canrail Pass for its entire network.

VIA-RAIL bookings in the UK: *Long-Haul Leisurerail; Box 113; Peterborough, Canada PE3 8HY; Tel: 01733/33 55 99.*

In Canada: *VIA Rail Canada, Tel: (800) 561-3949 or: Rocky Mountain Railtours; Tel: (800) 665-7245.*

VOLTAGE

Current is 110 V/60 Hz. You should Purchase an adapter before you leave home.

YOUTH HOSTELS

Canadian Hostelling Association hostels (a list of addresses can be found in the *Hostelling International Handbook, Volume 2; available from most bookstores or at any national association of youth hostels*) usually charge $6–22 per night per person. There are many hostels in particularly beautiful locations, for example in the National Parks in the Rocky Mountains (advance booking is required).

Information is also available on the Internet:
http://www.iyhf.org.
http://www.ymca.net.

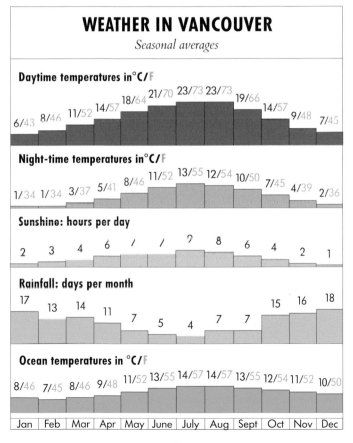

WEATHER IN VANCOUVER
Seasonal averages

Daytime temperatures in°C/F

6/43 8/46 11/52 14/57 18/64 21/70 23/73 23/73 19/66 14/57 9/48 7/45

Night-time temperatures in°C/F

1/34 1/34 3/37 5/41 8/46 11/52 13/55 12/54 10/50 7/45 4/39 2/36

Sunshine: hours per day

2 3 4 6 7 7 9 8 6 4 2 1

Rainfall: days per month

17 13 14 11 7 5 4 7 7 15 16 18

Ocean temperatures in °C/F

8/46 7/45 8/46 9/48 11/52 13/55 14/57 14/57 13/55 12/54 11/52 10/50

| Jan | Feb | Mar | Apr | May | June | July | Aug | Sept | Oct | Nov | Dec |

Do's and don'ts

*Some hints about possible dangers
and things you should avoid*

Don't decide to manage without travelinsurance

As foreigners you will generally be treated as private patients at the doctor's or at the hospital. A day in a Canadian clinic can easily cost you 1,000 dollars or more, so never travel without sufficient insurance.

Don't encourage thieves

Canada is a very safe country to travel in. The taxi drivers are honest. The attractions may not be cheap but they are worth the money. At the campsite you're more likely to have the necklace you left behind in the toilets returned to you than you are to be robbed in your mobile home. But it's the same here as anywhere. People are open to temptation in Canada too. So in the car park don't leave your camera in your car where it can be seen and don't walk down dark side streets on your own at night in the big cities.

Don't underestimate distances

Don't get your dimensions wrong in Canada. Especially in the far North a finger's width on the map can mean an enormously long day travelling on a gravel road.

Smoking

Smoking is as taboo in Canada as in the United States – and horrendously expensive at that. *No smoking* signs are no longer used these days. Smoking is automatically forbidden everywhere in public buildings, airports and restaurants and you should abide by this.

Don't hike in the wilderness without covering yourself

Whether you are going on a hike or a canoe trip in the wilderness for a day, a week or a month, you should always leave brief details of your route and the probable time of your return, either with the canoe rental firm, with the bush pilot who flew you into the wilderness, or with the *warden* at the National Park. Also any police station (RCMP) will be happy to take your details. If anything should go wrong, a search party can be sent out.

But don't forget to report in when you are back safely. And don't forget to take your mosquito repellent when going into the Canadian bush. Some *Off, Muskol* or *Cutter* will be sure to protect you from the greedy blood-suckers.

Road Atlas of Western Canada

*Please refer to back cover for an overview
of this road atlas*

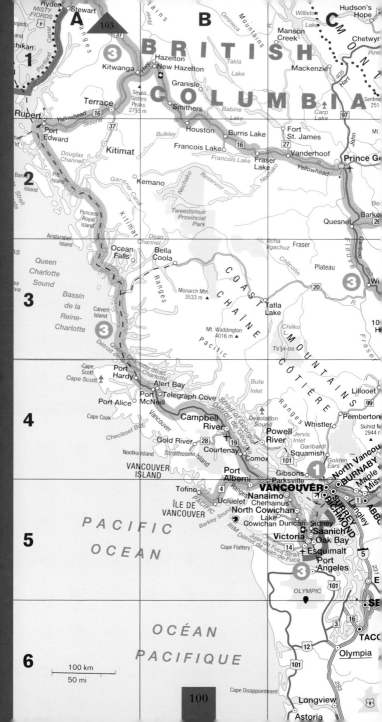

Hyder
MISTY
FIORDS
Stewart
A ▲103
37
Ranges
3
Kitwanga
Hazelton
New Hazelton
Hwy Hwy
Granisle

B R I T I S H

C O L U M B I A

Williston
Lake
Manson
Creek
Hudson's
Hope
Chetwyr
Pine
Mackenzie
Hart
Carp
Lake
97
Sentine
251

Terrace
16
Yellowhead
Skeena
37
Seven
Sisters
Peaks
2755 m
Smithers
Babine
Lake
Houston
Burns Lake
16
Fort
St. James
27
Vanderhoof
Yellowhead
John
Prince G
Mt.

Rupert
Port
Edward
Douglas
Channel
Bulkley
Francois Lake
Francois Lake
Fraser
Lake
Nechako

2
Kitimat
Kemano
Gardner Canal
Nechako
Reservoir
Nechako

Bank
Island
Pitt
Island
Princess
Royal
Island
Kitimat
Ranges
Dean
Channel
Tweedsmuir
Provincial
Park
Fraser
Quesnel
Barke
Bo

Aristazabel
Island
Ocean
Falls
Bella
Coola
Itcha
Ilgachuz
Chilcotin
Fraser
Fleuve
Plateau
3
Wi

Queen
Charlotte
Sound
Calvert
Island
Ranges
Monarch Mtn.
3533 m
C O A S T
Tatla
Lake
20
10
H

3
Bassin
de la
Reine-
Charlotte
3
Calvert
Island
Detroit de la Reine-Charlotte
Mt. Waddington
4016 m ▲
Chilko
L.
Ts'yl-ps
Pacific
C H A Î N E
M O U N T A I N S
C Ô T I È R E
Fraser

Cape
Scott
Cape Scott
Port
Hardy
Port
McNeill
Alert Bay
Telegraph Cove
Bute
Inlet
Lillooet
99

4
Port Alice
Cape Cook
Checleset Bay
Campbell
River
Vancouver
Gold River
28
Courtenay
19
Desolation
Sound
Powell
River
101
Jervis
Inlet
Garibaldi
Squamish
Whistler
Pemberton
Skihist M
2944 r
Nootka Island
Strathcona
Provincial
Park
Comox
Golden
Ears
North Vancou
1
BURNABY
Maple
Miss

VANCOUVER ISLAND
Port
Alberni
Gibsons
Parksville
VANCOUVER
RICHMOND
Langley
ABB
1

Tofino
Ucluelet
4
PACIFIC
Ranges
Nanaimo
Chemainus
North Cowichan
Cowichan
Lake
Duncan
Saanich
Sidney
Oak Bay
2311
E

5
P A C I F I C

O C E A N
Barkley Sound
ÎLE DE
VANCOUVER
RIM Détroit de Juan-de-Fuca
Juan de Fuca Strait
Cape Flattery
Victoria
Esquimalt
Port
Angeles
14
5
SE

3
OLYMPIC
101
TAC

6
O C É A N

P A C I F I Q U E
100 km
50 mi
12
Olympia
3
16
101
293
Cape Disappointment
Longview
Astoria
8
100

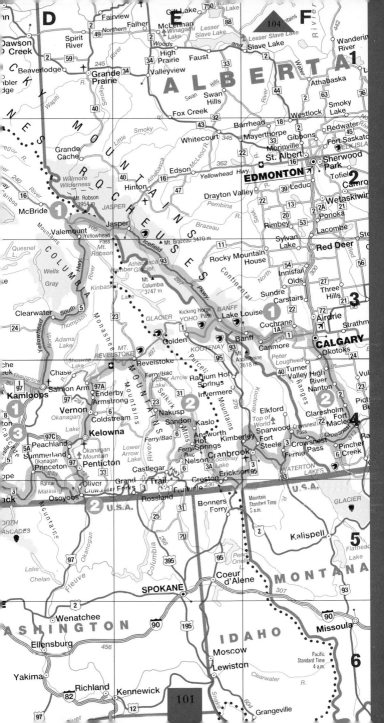

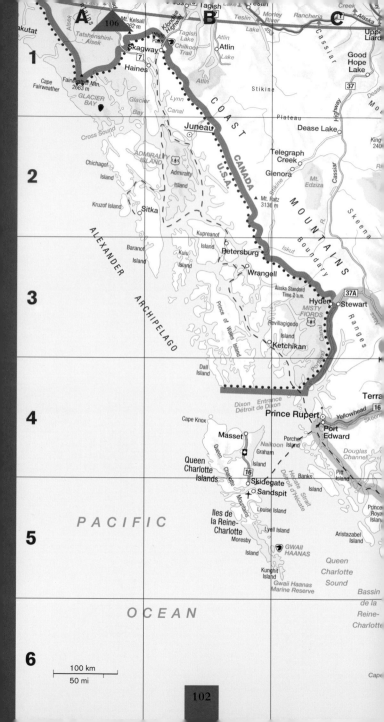

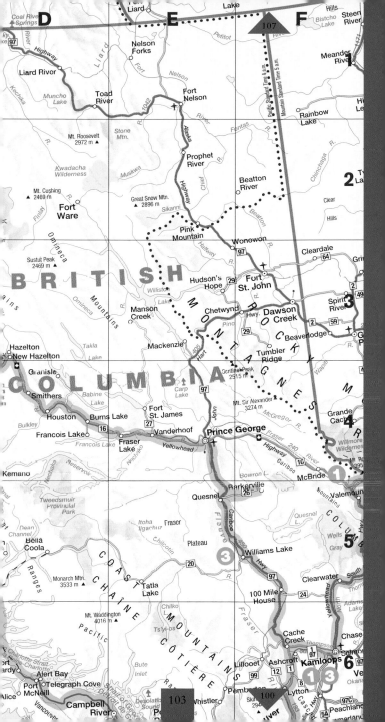

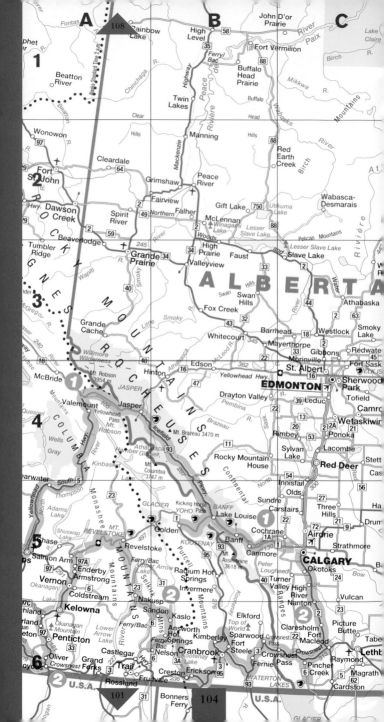

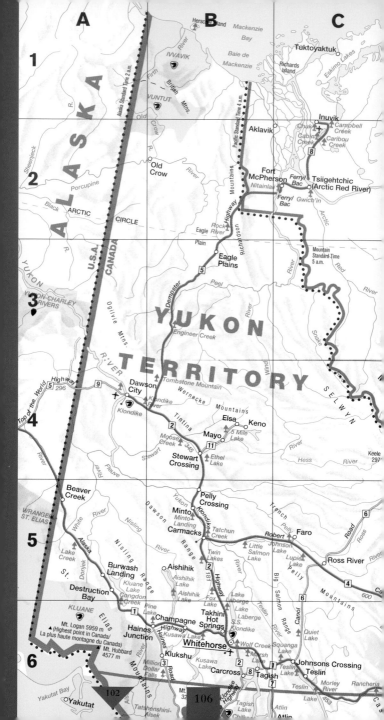

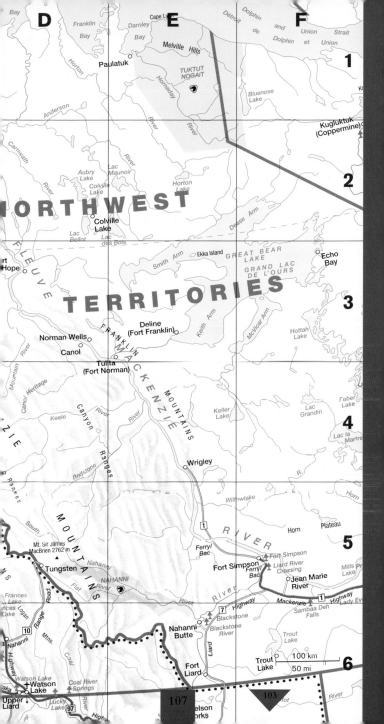

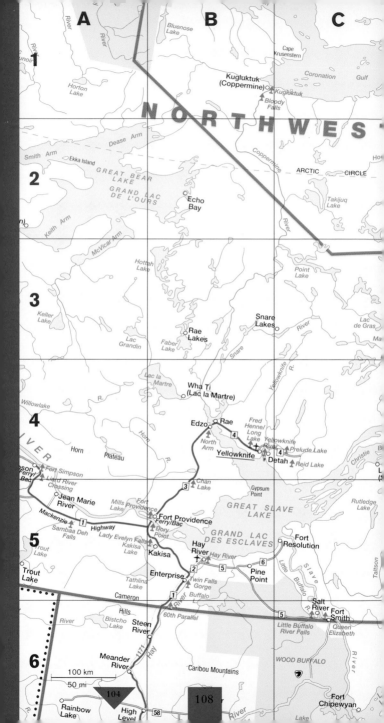

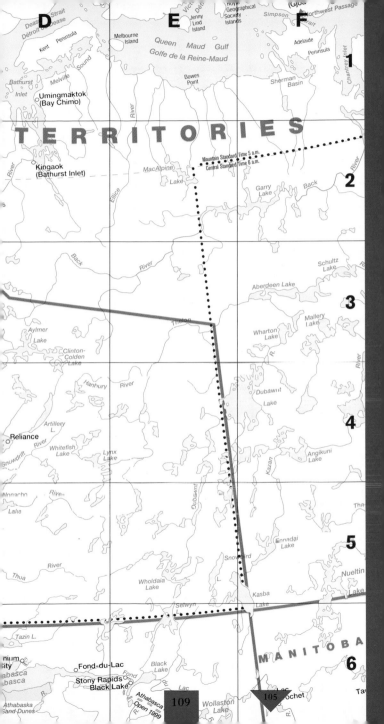

ROAD ATLAS LEGEND

Trans-Kanada-Highway	🔷	Trans-Canada Highway
Gebührenpflichtige Autobahn	81	Toll Expressway
Autobahn	16	Expressway (Limited Access)
Interstate Highway (U.S.A.)	90	Interstate Highway (U.S.A.)
Hauptverbindungsstraße	5 93	Principal Highway
Nebenstraße	10	Secondary Highway
Sonstige Straßen		Local Road
Entfernung in Kilometer	⟋ 382 ⟍	Distance in kilometres
Eisenbahn		Railway
Fähre	– – – – –	Ferry
Zeitzonengrenze	• • • • • • • •	Time zone boundary
Provinzpark	Cape Scott 🔺	Provincial park
Nationalpark	BANFF 🛡	National park
Internationale Grenze		International boundary
Provinz- oder Bundesstaatengrenze		Provincial, territorial or state boundary
Provinz- oder Territorialgrenze, unmarkiert	▬ ▬ ▬ ▬ ▬	Provincial, territorial boundary, undemarcated
Territoriale Gebietsgrenze		Territorial district boundary
Provinzhauptstadt	**QUÉBEC**	Provincial capital
Einwohnerzahl unter 10 000	○ Cobalt	Population less than 10 000
Einwohnerzahl zwischen 10 000 und 50 000	⊙ Lethbridge	Population 10 000 to 50 000
Einwohnerzahl zwischen 50 000 und 100 000	◎ **Markham**	Population 50 000 to 100 000
Einwohnerzahl zwischen 100 000 und 500 000	◉ **LAVAL**	Population 100 000 to 500 000
Einwohnerzahl zwischen 500 000 und 1 000 000	◉ **CALGARY**	Population 500 000 to 1 000 000
Einwohnerzahl über 1 000 000	■ **TORONTO**	Population greater than 1 000 000
Stadtgebiet		Built-up area

```
        100 miles
├─────────────────┤
    100 km
```

Also by Melissa Mayhue

Thirty Nights with a Highland Husband

Highland Guardian

Soul of a Highlander

A Highlander of Her Own

A Highlander's Destiny